“打开经济学之门”
原版注释基础读本

U0611700

管理学基础——原理篇

MANAGEMENT：THE BASICS

（注释版）

（英）摩根·威策尔　著

刘清江　吴鹏昊　译注

经济科学出版社

图书在版编目（CIP）数据

管理学基础. 原理篇：英文／（英）威策尔著；刘清江，吴鹏昊译. —北京：经济科学出版社，2011.8
（"打开经济学之门"原版注释基础读本）
ISBN 978 - 7 - 5141 - 0913 - 9

Ⅰ.①管… Ⅱ.①威… ②刘… ③吴… Ⅲ.①管理学－英文 Ⅳ.①C93

中国版本图书馆 CIP 数据核字（2011）第 156240 号

责任编辑：龚　勋　吴鹏昊
责任校对：徐领柱
版式设计：代小卫
技术编辑：王世伟

管理学基础——原理篇
（注释版）

（英）摩根·威策尔　著

刘清江　吴鹏昊　译注

经济科学出版社出版、发行　新华书店经销
社址：北京市海淀区阜成路甲 28 号　邮编：100142
总编部电话：88191217　发行部电话：88191540
网址：www. esp. com. cn
电子邮件：esp@ esp. com. cn
北京中科印刷有限公司印装
787×1092　16 开　15.75 印张　351000 字
2011 年 12 月第 1 版　2011 年 12 月第 1 次印刷
ISBN 978 - 7 - 5141 - 0913 - 9　定价：36.00 元

策 划 人 语

　　《"打开经济学之门"原版注释基础读本》系列丛书是经济科学出版社适应新形势下高校双语教学需求的精心策划之作。

　　秉承经济科学出版社"繁荣经济科学，宣传服务财政"的办社宗旨，丛书的策划者从中国读者的英文阅读实际水平出发，从海量的国外教材和教辅书中挑选了广义经济学的八本入门读本，内容涵盖经济学、管理学、金融学、营销学等门类，编写体例分为原理篇、概念篇和人物篇三大类，原理篇旨在介绍该学科最基础的理论框架；概念篇则一一介绍该学科最核心的概念；同时，丛书的另外一大创新是：还尝试着加入了人物篇，例如，《管理学基础——人物篇》介绍了自文艺复兴时期以来的 50 位著名的管理学大师的生平和思想。丛书力图通过原理、概念、人物的多角度、多层面呈现，为初涉经济学领域的青年学子和所有非经济学专业的读者们立体地勾画出一幅完整的学术图景，而且是原汁原味的呈现。

　　《"打开经济学之门"原版注释基础读本》系列丛书被设计成开放式结构：我们将根据读者的反馈逐渐地出版更多的切合中国读者需求的好作品。丛书知识性和趣味性并重，英文通俗易懂，适合大学本科低年级学生、高职高专学生阅读。

　　丛书的初衷是出版中文翻译版本，然而在漫长的试译、翻译、校译过程中，一方面是深感语言传达的艰难，另一方面是考虑到时至 21 世纪，中国读者的英文阅读水平早已经超越了出版者的预期，读者对译文标准性的挑剔也成为出版者的新高度，从而逐渐萌发了出版注释版的想法：为读者提供全英文的读本，只加上少量的中文注解。通过与国外出版者艰难的谈判，最终成功地说服了外方，获得了在中国出版英文注释版的独家授权。为此，我们付出了超出预期好几倍的辛劳。

然而，这仅仅只是开始，读者的接受和喜欢才是我们最终的目标。希望读者喜欢我们的创意，为我们提供更多的创意！

2011 年 11 月

目　　录

WHAT IS MANAGEMENT?

什么是管理

You read a book from beginning to end. You run a business the opposite way. You start with the end, and then do everything you must to reach it.

(Harold Geneen)

读一本书是从头到尾，而做生意却沿着相反的路。你带着目标开始，然后尽力去实现。

——哈罗德·吉宁

Management is the co-ordination and the direction of the activities of oneself and others towards some particular end. For the purposes of this book, we take this end to be the running of a business, but it should be recognized that management exists in other organizations and fields of activity as well. The provision of health care and education, the running of government departments and the armed forces, and the operation of charitable organizations, for example, all require some degree of management. But because the problems and tasks of management in those other organizations are in many ways quite similar to those of businesses, we will take the commercial business as our main focus.

The word 'management' is quite an old one. Its origins lie in the Latin *manus*, meaning literally 'by hand' but also 'power' and 'jurisdiction'. By the later Middle Ages the Italian word *maneggiare* had appeared, referring to any official in charge of a production facility, such as a cloth manufacturing workshop, or an overseas trading office. This word evolved into the French *manegerie* and then the English 'management', which is first recorded in a document of 1589. By the end of the seventeenth century, the words 'manager' and 'management' were in common English usage, and it was recognized that business organizations employed people whose primary job was to supervise the activities of others.

Although managers have existed for a long time, the idea that 'management' can be studied and taught is a relatively new one. Not until the very end of the nineteenth century did this idea begin to develop in any detail. The scientific revolution of the nineteenth century pervaded all walks of life, with an ethos that life could be improved if its various aspects could be studied and analyzed in detail. Studies of management began first in the workplace, with engineers like Frederick Winslow Taylor, Harrington Emerson and Henri Fayol developing detailed formal theories of management, and then in academia, with the establishment of business schools in the USA at Dartmouth College, the University of Pennsylvania, and then most famously at Harvard University in 1908. From there the formal study of management grew steadily, developing an immense body of theoretical and practical knowledge.

The size of this body of knowledge—the online bookseller Amazon. com lists 32, 000 books on management, and the number of journal articles runs into the millions—can be more than a little daunting for the first-time student. However, many of these books and articles are highly specialized, looking only at one small part or aspect of management. Although valuable contributions to the theory and practice of management, these will be difficult if not impossible to understand without at least some background knowledge of what management is and how it functions.

The aim of this book is to provide some, at least, of that

background knowledge by exploring the 'basics' of management. Having said what management is, we should now explain what we mean by 'basics'. Although much of management is complex and technical, it is also possible to reduce the study and practice of management to a relatively small number of fundamental ideas and concepts. These 'basics' are things that are part of all business management, no matter where the business is or what kind of business it is. For example, management has to consider the following:

- Every business needs a set of goals and a strategy for getting there. Without goals and a coherent strategy, much effort will be wasted.
- Every business needs an organization which will pull together resources and people to meet those goals.
- Every organization is made up of people, whose work needs to be guided and co-ordinated. These people all have their own needs and aspirations, which must be accommodated within the organization.
- Every business requires customers if it is to sell its products and services and earn money.
- Every business needs to have something to sell, products and services, if it is to have customers.
- Every business has to manage its money, both that received as income from customers and that put into the business by investors.
- Every business depends on knowledge; without it, people cannot be managed, customers cannot be found and products cannot be made.
- Every business is to some extent affected by culture, both the culture that develops within the organization and the national or local culture of the environment within which it operates.

It must be added that these 'basics' do not create themselves. Strategy does not emerge out of nowhere; someone actually has to sit down and decide what it is to be. Organizations do not build themselves; someone has to provide the catalyst for them. It is these sorts of basic tasks that form the roles and responsibilities of the manager.

As expressed above, these roles and responsibilities look simple. And at heart, they are. However, just because something is simple does not mean that it is easy. To say that businesses need customers is to state a simple truth; to actually go out and get customers is another matter. Fortunately, there are other 'basics' that we can use to guide us as well. In terms of customers, we can start with a fundamental premise that all customers have needs and wants that they are trying to satisfy. It follows that if we as managers can understand those needs and wants, then we can design products and services that will attract customers and persuade them to buy from us. The study of marketing offers many different ways of doing these things, but it all boils down to the same thing: identify potential customers, learn their needs, then make products and provide services that they want at a price they can afford and that will make a profit for the company. Keeping this basic principle in mind will help make the rest of the study of marketing seem much more clear.

Each chapter in this book goes on to explain the basics of the various major disciplines of management-strategy, organization, human resource management, marketing, production and finance-and then the basics of a few all-embracing influences like knowledge and culture. Before we get into these, however, let us look at a few 'basics of the basics', concepts that underpin all the more specific terms which are used throughout the book.

WHAT MANAGERS DO
管理者该做什么

The above shows what managers are responsible for, but

what exactly do managers do on a day-to-day basis? The problem is that when asked, managers themselves often have trouble describing what it is they do. Researchers such as Henry Mintzberg and Warren Bennis, who have made detailed studies of how managers do their work, speak of the *ad hoc* nature of management and how managers spend much of their time dealing with situations as they arise rather than working through structured lists of tasks and processes. So, any description of what managers do has to be treated with caution, because different managers do different things at different times.

A number of attempts have been made to draw up lists of tasks that managers carry out. The French engineer Henri Fayol divided managerial work into five categories: (1) forecasting and planning, (2) building organizations and systems, (3) directing subordinates, (4) co-ordinating various activities across the business, and (5) guiding these activities so that all parts of the business are working towards the same end. One of the most famous management writers, the American Peter Drucker, also provides five categories: (1) setting objectives, (2) organizing, (3) motivating and communicating, (4) measurement of work accomplished and (5) developing people. There are a number of similarities in the two lists, although there are a few differences as well. Neither list should be taken as absolutely complete, but both give an idea of the nature of managerial work.

At an even more basic level, all the activities described by Fayol and Drucker can be reduced to a few building blocks. In any given situation, what managers ideally do is the following. First, they analyze information and understand what needs doing. Second, they plan what is to be done and decide or agree who will do it. Third, they co-ordinate the resources necessary to carry out the plan and ensure that it is being carried out. Fourth, they look at the results, decide whether the plan was successful and, if not, what further action needs to be taken.

Again, this is simple, but it is not easy. This is particularly the case given that most managers work under severe time pressures and are nearly always doing more than one thing at a time. A dozen or more issues may command their attention simultaneously. There may not be enough time for detailed analysis and planning: snap decisions made in a few seconds may be necessary. It is for this reason that many writers caution against an overly rational approach to management. Another American writer, Chester Barnard, believed that the key traits of a successful manager were not so much the ability to reason scientifically, but things like feeling, judgement, sense, proportion and balance. Another of the basics of management, then, is that common sense and judgement are critical to the role.

THE PURPOSE OF MANAGEMENT
管理的宗旨

Managers do these things, of course, not because they are ends in themselves, but because the business requires it. Let us briefly state two concepts (we will develop these concepts in more detail later in the book, in chapters 2 and 7). First, every business has to have goals. These can be many and various, and can include growing or increasing sales, growing or increasing the size of the market, providing more value for shareholders, providing greater benefit to consumers, and so on. A business must have such goals; without them, efforts lose focus and the business will no longer be able to compete with more focused and directed rivals.

Second, although the reaching of goals is the responsibility of managers, and they will probably also have primary responsibility for deciding what those goals will be, unless managers themselves own shares or are partners in the business, they do not own the company. It is not theirs; it belongs, legally and morally, to the shareholders who have provided the money to establish the business and allow it to grow. Managers are stewards or custodians. They work for the benefit of the company, and are rewarded for their work with a salary and other benefits. But they must not act in a way which is against the interests of the owners of the company. If they do so, they may be acting unethically, and in many jurisdictions they may also be guilty of offences against the law. For example, in the late 1990s senior managers at Enron and other companies took decisions which increased the share price of those companies, thereby enriching themselves through bonuses and share options, but which proved to be very detrimental to the companies themselves and their owners. Some of those managers have now been prosecuted.

The purpose of management is to carry out the tasks needed to enable the business to reach its goals. But managers are also usually charged by the shareholders with setting those goals themselves. They thus have a dual set of responsibilities: to set realistic goals which the company can meet and which will benefit the owners of the company, and then to ensure those goals are met as planned.

DEFINITIONS 定义

Some of the following terms will be found throughout this book, and an understanding of them will help make later concepts seem more clear.

Capital   Capital usually means money invested in the 资本 business, although some theorists talk of the organizational strengths of the business and its accumulated knowledge as forms of capital. Capital is an 'input', and is necessary to transform resources (below) into finished goods and services which can be sold to customers. For example, capital is necessary to buy machinery and set up a factory in order to make cars.

效果　　*Effectiveness*　Effectiveness is a measure of how well a business—or a person—is meeting its goals. If the goal is to provide high-quality products that customers want, and the business is succeeding in doing so, then the business is working effectively. If products are poor and customers do not want them, then the business is not being effective.

效率　　*Efficiency*　Efficiency is a measure of how well a business—or a person—is using resources. If money and materials are being used well and there is little waste, then the business is working efficiently. If costs are too high or raw materials are being wasted, then the business is said to be inefficient. Exactly what constitutes efficiency varies from business to business and the kinds of products or services being produced.

企业家精神　　*Entrepreneurship*　Entrepreneurship is a collective term for a set of behaviours and actions associated particularly with the setting up of new businesses, but sometimes found within previously existing organizations as well. Entrepreneurship has strong connotations of creativity and risk-taking; people described as entrepreneurs tend to be both highly imaginative and willing to accept higher than usual levels of risk. Management academics do not always agree that entrepreneurship should be included as part of management, as management is often seen as aiming to control and limit risk. However, companies tend to appreciate entrepreneurial qualities in their managers.

环境　　*Environment*　Environment, in business terms, is the place, time and culture in which the company operates. Many forces in the environment will have an effect on the business, including competition (how many other companies are in the same or similar business, and what are they doing), regulation (how does government treat business and what laws govern its conduct), economics (how strong/weak is demand for goods generally) and more general social issues such as concern for the physical environment, social justice and so on. The factors in the environment are nearly always outside the control of managers, and they are often forced to respond to these at the same time as planning for the business itself.

Growth   Growth is a general term which can mean either 增长
expanding the size of the business (numbers of employees, volume of goods made and sold) or the value of the business, that is to say, the value of its assets and the work it is carrying out. Chapter 7 gives more on how the value of a business is calculated.

Income   Income, or revenue, is money the business 收益
brings in through the sale of its products and services. This is one of two ways money can be brought into a business; the other is through invested capital (see above).

Innovation   Innovation can be the development of either 创新
new products and services to sell to customers, or new ways of making products and services that reduce costs or increase efficiency (or both). Innovation is in turn dependent on knowledge (see Chapter 8).

Leadership   Leadership is often distinguished from man- 领导
agement, in that the main purpose of the leader is to set general goals and then inspire the rest of the organization to move towards those goals; detailed planning and execution are not properly the province of the leader. Leadership is, however, necessary in some aspects of management, particularly in the management of change (see chapters 3 and 9).

Profit   Profit is the excess of income over expenditure. If 利润
a business is bringing in more income than it is spending, then it is making a profit; if not, then it is making a loss. Remember that money invested as capital does not count as income, and is not included in the calculation of profit.

Resources   Resources are what a business requires in 资源
addition to capital in order to make and sell things. Resources include raw materials and parts from which products are built; human labour and knowledge to make the products; and tech-

nology (see below) to assist in making and delivering them. It is sometimes said that resources are only 'potential', and not realised until capital is provided as a catalyst to turn them into actual goods and services.

技术

Technology Technology includes mechanical and electronic devices which are used to design, make and deliver products and services to customers, or to support other organizational tasks such as communication and co-ordination. Strictly speaking, any artefact used by people at work, such as a hammer or a saw, is technology. At the time of writing, the most widespread and powerful form of technology is the desktop or laptop computer linked to the Internet.

价值

Value Value is what the business puts into the products and services it makes and sells. A collection of parts or a barrel of raw materials has a certain value on it; the business, by combining labour, parts, materials and technology, produces a finished product or service that has a value greater than the sum of all those parts. It is this value that attracts customers (who otherwise would buy the parts and make the product themselves). The process of building in value by the business is known as the value chain.

With these terms in mind, let us now move directly to the first function of management, the setting of goals and the development of strategies for meeting them.

摘要

● 管理是指为实现既定目标而对自己和他人的活动进行的协调和指导。

● 管理的宗旨是执行使企业达到它的目标而需要的任务。

● 尽管在许多方面高度复杂，管理仍然可以浓缩成简单的基本思想和概念，即基础知识。这些基础知识存在于所有企业管理中，无论企业在哪里或者是何种企业。

SUGGESTIONS FOR FURTHER READING
延伸阅读

Bennis, W., *Managing People is Like Herding Cats*, Provo, UT: Executive Excellence Publishing, 1997.

An easy read and well worth a look; despite its title, the book is about management generally, not just managing people.

Drucker, P., *Management: Tasks, Responsibilities, Practices*, New York: Harper & Row, 1974.

A classic by one of the all-time great management gurus, this is a big book and takes a while to get through. The definitions of management, however, remain influential. Alternatively, try the shorter essays in Drucker's The New Realities (*New York: Harper & Row*, 1989)*, especially those on management and the liberal arts.*

Fayol, H., *General and Industrial Management*, trans. I. Gray, New York: David S. Lake, 1984.

An early attempt (the book was first published in 1917*) to construct a general theory of what management is, this book has indirectly influenced much modern thinking about management.*

Grove, A., *High Output Management*, New York: Random House, 1983.

An attempt to explain what management is and what managers do in simple terms, by a very successful senior manager. Grove's other book, Only the Paranoid Survive, *is also worth reading, but this is a very good introduction to the subject.*

Mintzberg, H., *The Nature of Managerial Work*, New York, Harper & Row, 1973.

This was a revolutionary book in its day, and still runs counter to much formal management theory. The picture of how managers actually do management, however, remains a compelling one.

2

STRATEGY

战　略

Everything in strategy is very simple, but that does not mean that everything in strategy is very easy.

（Karl von Clausewitz）

战略之中诸事简单，却非事事容易。

——卡尔·冯·克劳塞维茨

The term 'strategy' refers to the plans a business makes in order to determine how it will reach its goals. That definition is deliberately broad, and anyone reading more deeply into this subject will quickly see that there are widely differing views as to what strategy is, and is not. We will touch on some of these arguments below, but for now, let us assume that strategy is the process of doing the following:

- determining what goals the business should have;
- determining what options exist for reaching those goals;
- choosing the best available option;
- putting the plan into practice so as to reach the desired goal.

Because strategy in effect tells what the business is going to do and how it is going to do it, the subject is of very great importance. Most business schools now teach business strategy as a core course, requiring all students to take it; some even make it the first course on the curriculum, so that students begin studying strategy on day 1. Other courses in areas such as marketing, human resource management, technology management and so on will usually have a strong element of strategy built into them.

DEFINITIONS 定义

Before going further, there are a few concepts that need to be defined.

Mission　The mission of the business is a statement of 使命 what that business believes to be its guiding purpose and ethos. Often missions are set out in a formal mission statement, which is given to all employees. Missions are statements of intent or belief, and are not necessarily concrete goals as such.

Goals　Goals, or targets, are firm statements of the posi- 目标 tion where the company would like to be. They are often expressed numerically. Common business goals include:

- increasing income, sales and/or profits by a specified percentage or amount over a specified time. For example, 'We want to increase our turnover by 15 per cent over the next two years.'

- increasing market share to a specified level, such as: 'We want to have 30 per cent of the market in two years' time.' Simply, this means that the company wants to ensure that 30 per cent of all customers in a particular market are buying its products rather than those of its rivals.

- growing the market to a specified level, such as: 'We want to grow the market by 10 per cent over the next two years.' This means that the company wants to increase the numbers of its own customers by 10 per cent, regardless of what its rivals might be doing.

Strategic objectives　Strategic objectives can be thought of as 战略目标 staging posts towards goals. Achieving a complex goal such as increasing turnover or growing a market requires many different activities by many parts of the business. To achieve turnover growth may require investment in new resources and hiring new employees. New products and new technology systems will be required. Marketing teams will need to find new customers, or increase demand by existing ones. Thus each part of the business ends up with its own set of objectives, which taken all together add up to the overall business goal. This means, of course, that as well as the overall strategy of the business, there will be many different 'mini-strategies' going on in various parts of the business so that these individual objectives can be achieved.

战略选择

Strategic options　Strategy is never black and white. When choosing a strategy, there are always at least three options—do this, do something else, or do nothing—and usually there are very many more than that. At first glance, it is not always clear which choice will be the best. Nor are some options always immediately obvious. Working out what the options are and choosing the best one is the second most difficult and risky part of strategy (the most difficult is implementing the strategy, which we will come onto in a moment). Picking the right option could lead to long-term success, but picking the wrong one can result in expensive failure.

战略限制

Strategic constraints　In a perfect world, we would always pick the ideal option for ourselves and our businesses. But in reality, what looks like the ideal option sometimes turns out not to be possible. When choosing a strategy, large or small, managers have to look at the following issues:

- Time: can the strategy be developed and put into place in time to meet its goals?
- Cost: can the business actually afford the costs of implementing this particular strategy?
- Resources: does the business have the skills and resources to carry out this strategy successfully?
- Internal factors: is this strategy going to be acceptable to the company's employees?

- Ethical and legal considerations: is this strategy going to be acceptable to government and to society?

If the answer to any of the above is 'no', then managers will probably have to start looking at new options.

Core competencies　The strategies a business can adopt and, realistically, put into effect will be limited by the resources the business has available; not just money, but also talent, ability and knowledge on the part of employees. The Red Cross is a humanitarian organization with many medical staff and others trained in relief work. Realistically, its best and most effective strategies will be focused on humanitarian aid. The Red Cross could not develop and carry out an effective strategy for, let us say, launching manned space missions, because it lacks the core competencies this requires (though whether it might still do a better job of this than NASA is an arguable point).

核心竞争力

Implementation　Very simply, implementation refers to the process of making strategy work, of carrying out the plan to its conclusion. This is the most difficult and risky part of all strategy, and the area where most strategic failures occur. We will talk about this in more detail later in the chapter.

实施

THE ORIGINS OF BUSINESS STRATEGY 企业战略的起源

Strategy is a term adopted into management from military science. The word comes from the Greek *strategia*, where it referred loosely to the art and science of war (in the Byzantine Empire, the word for 'general' was *strategos*). In ancient China, the general Sunzi, or Sun Tzu, produced his *The Art of War* around the fifth century BC. The book (which was heavily rewritten in the 3rd century AD) became standard reading for both soldiers and businesspeople in East Asia, and also more recently in the West.

In Europe, the sixteenth-century Florentine politician and writer Niccolò Machiavelli outlined his view of strategy in several books, including *The Prince*. Machiavelli believed that there were two key components in any strategy: *virtù*, or the resolve and strength that a leader showed in carrying a plan through, and *fortuna*, meaning serendipity or luck. *Fortuna* could not be controlled, but it could be anticipated and taken advantage of. His ideas were picked up by two German writers of the nineteenth century, the Prussian staff officer Karl von Clausewitz, who fought against Napoleon, and Field Marshal Helmuth von Moltke, the Prussian general who defeated France in the war of 1870 – 71. Both men thought that there were some basic principles of strategy which could lead to success, but emphasized that no strategy could be *guaranteed* to succeed. They referred to the concept of 'friction', a combination of small but unforeseen events which slowly builds up and creates pressure and distractions for the leader. These can prompt the leader to deviate from the strategy or even abandon it altogether; Moltke once famously commented that 'no plan survives contact with the enemy'. Overcoming friction requires strength and resolve to carry a plan through. In other words, implementation is as important as the strategy itself.

These two ideas, of generic strategies and of the importance of implementation, were carried over into the world of business in the early twentieth century. The management thinkers of that period borrowed heavily from other disciplines, and they greatly admired Moltke as a strategist and organizer. Until the 1960s, business strategy was virtually a wholesale transfer of the principles of military strategy into the business world, and that influence remains strong today (witness the popularity of books like *Marketing Warfare*).

Business strategy remains a developing and evolving field. Many of the major theoretical debates—on the relationship between strategy and goals, on the relationship between strategy and organization, on the relevance of generic strategies—have not yet been resolved. It is important to be aware of these debates when studying strategies, and to note the positions which individual authors take when writing about them.

GENERIC STRATEGIES 一般竞争战略

The idea that there are generic strategies in business comes also from military science, and has met with a good reception. Generals like tried and proven recipes for success that they can employ in any situation, and so do business managers.

BOX 2.1 SOME COMMON GENERIC STRATEGIES

- *Grow* -the first priority of the business is to achieve growth.
- *Defend* -the business reckons the prospects for growth are poor, and will instead seek to defend its existing position against rivals.
- *Harvest* -the business feels the market is stable or declining, and will seek to make as much money as possible while the situation lasts.
- *Divest* —the business feels the market has no future, and gets out.
- *Turnaround* —the business itself has been struggling but there is still potential in the market; the task now is to reorganize and seek to reclaim lost market share, turnover, etc.

One of the most famous sets of generic strategies is that developed by Michael Porter in his book *Competitive Strategy* (1980). Porter held that all businesses have just four basic strategic options open to them:

1. *Cost leadership*: selling goods to a mass market at a lower price than rivals;

2. *Differentiation*: selling goods to a mass market that are superior in quality to those of rivals;

3. *Cost focus*: selling goods to a small, narrowly defined market at a lower price than rivals;

4. *Focused differentiation*: selling goods to a small, narrowly defined market that are superior in quality to those of rivals.

The only two decisions the company needs to make, says Professor Porter, are whether to sell to a mass market or to a small one (competitive scope) and whether to compete on the basis of price or on the basis of product features and quality (competitive advantage). All else will follow.

Proponents of generic strategies argue that the best strategies are the simplest ones. All business goals are fundamentally similar—to increase turnover, to increase market share, and so on—and the strategic requirements of any given situation are at heart similar as well. Only a limited number of strategic options will be effective in a given situation. So, rather than reinventing the wheel every time, they need to develop a new strategy, managers can analyze the situation, decide which generic option best fits their needs and then customize it as the situation might require.

Opponents of generic strategies concede that they are easy to use, but argue that this creates a mental trap. Managers develop a mindset where they are unwilling to look beyond the generic strategies that have been presented to them, or to think critically about whether there might be other options. Other opponents reject the idea that all business situations are similar, and argue instead that ongoing changes in the business environment are rendering old strategic options obsolete. With the very ways that we do business, contact customers, manage employees and so on changing all the time, how can we possibly apply the same old strategies?

'Generic strategies' ought more properly to be described as 'generic strategic options'. It is true to say that in any given situation the number of choices is limited, and the kind of strategic options shown in Box 2.1 above make useful starting points. It is also true—and this is another lesson learned from military science—that the best strategies are very often the simplest. Strategies are like machines; those with the smallest number of moving parts are least likely to break down. At the same time, simplification does reduce options. Making strategy is ultimately a creative process, and keeping an open mind about new possibilities outside the 'box' of conventional thinking is very important.

The problem comes when we start to think about generic strategies as *rules* rather than principles. If we see these kinds of strategies as rulebooks that we have to follow, and see any deviation from them as being unsound or wrong, then we do risk inhibiting creative approaches and missing out on new opportunities. A useful precept to follow here might be the advice of the British novelist Evelyn Waugh, who once wrote: 'I regard rules as useful guides as to how to misbehave most effectively.' Generic strategies/strategic options are a valuable starting point, but often their real value lies in showing you how best to deviate from them.

STEPS IN BUSINESS STRATEGY 商业战略实施步骤

It may be difficult to find formulas for strategy itself, but there is a fairly simple, tried and tested process for developing strategy. The following procedures, with some variation, will be found in most business textbooks.

EVALUATION 评估

The process begins by looking at the business itself. What is its current state? How well is it performing? What are its strengths, and its weaknesses? Sometimes this process has to go further and ask some really visceral questions like, what does this business do? Who are its customers? What is its basic purpose? This can lead to re-evaluation of the business goals and even of the mission itself, though some management writers are convinced that setting goals and mission should be kept separate from strategy. At all events, the first step in strategy is to make sure that the manager has a clear picture of the business, what it can do and what its limitations are.

SCANNING THE ENVIRONMENT 环境分析

The next step is to look at the environment. When we talk of environment we do not specifically mean the natural environment or the geosphere, although the condition of these will often be important. Environment, in this context, means the entire world external to the business: its customers, its suppliers, the current attitude of government and regulatory bodies, the activities of any competitors, general social trends, international and domestic political trends, overall market trends and so on. All of these have to be analyzed and understood. Some companies, especially large ones, conduct this kind of environmental scanning on a constant basis, updating their own knowledge about their environment all the time. Others, with fewer resources, are forced to conduct formal scanning exercises periodically. But individual managers can do some scanning for themselves on a daily basis, even by such simple means as reading newspapers and the trade press.

DEFINING STRATEGIC PRIORITIES
界定战略优先权

Evaluating the position tells the manager what strengths and weaknesses the company has, while scanning the environment shows what opportunities may lie in the market—and also what threats to the business may exist or be developing (new competitors could be coming in, prices of raw materials could be going up and eating into profits, etc.). Once a composite picture of all these has been assembled, it is possible to determine what the strategic priorities should be. What needs to be done most urgently to reach goals? What problems need to be dealt with? What opportunities need to be taken advantage of?

DEFINING AND ASSESSING STRATE-
GIC OPTIONS　确定和评估战略选择

Defining options can be time-consuming, frustrating and risky. This is a critical stage; picking the wrong option can send the company down the wrong road, and rectifying the mistake later can be very costly. Nor will the nature of each option always be clear. Some will be obviously wrong; others may appear to be right; still others will be unclear. Sometimes two or more options will appear to be equally 'right' and management teams can then spend hours or even days arguing over which 'right' option to pick: like the donkey in the Greek fable that starved to death because it could not make up its mind which of two equally tempting bunches of hay to eat. Always remember during this stage that a decision *must* be made, and a second-best decision is usually better than no decision at all.

For those who are really stuck at this stage, the generic options we mentioned above can come in useful here. They can, at least, provide a starting point for more detailed thinking. By comparing generic options to the real situation—as determined in the previous two stages—one can adapt the former to arrive at some realistic alternatives. Valuable time can often be saved in this way.

For those who want to reject generic options in favour of the more creative approach, it is still necessary to be systematic. The first step is to make sure that all involved understand and agree on the fundamental problem or issue. If, for example, the goal that has been agreed on is to increase turnover by 10 per cent over two years, then start with that premise. Next, look at every area of the business, even the most peripheral to the current issue. In what ways can that area contribute to increasing turnover? This generates a starting list of options. Some of these will rule themselves out almost immediately as being costly or impractical. But by considering and analyzing the remainder and whittling them down, one can fairly quickly arrive at a range of practical options. The American consultant William J. Altier recommends scoring options on a scale of 1 – 10 based on how ' satisfactory' the management team considers each to be. This stage also involves considering what resources will be needed to put the strategy into effect; resources and costs will be a very important factor in determining the viability of each option.

The final choice may be as much subjective as objective, particularly where two more equally satisfactory options present themselves. A subjective element is always present in strategy-making.

SETTING OBJECTIVES AND TARGETS 设定目的和目标

With the strategic option chosen, there comes the stage of setting intermediate objectives and targets for different areas and departments of the business. This setting of detailed targets helps make clear to everyone in the business what their own responsibility will be.

PLANNING WAYS AND MEANS
规划方法和手段

The overall strategic framework is now in place, and the next step is to plan how each goal will be reached. More detailed resource requirements can be drawn up, and budgets can be established for each stage of implementation. This is really a continuation of the previous stage, but involves planning at a more detailed level.

PLANNING FOR CONTINGENCY AND RISK 应急规划和风险

What happens if the strategy goes wrong? If 'friction' builds up, then the whole strategy risks being thrown off course. All sorts of things can of course go wrong, ranging from costs being higher than expected, to major disasters such as fire, terrorism or war. The list of things that can go wrong is literally endless, and could cause sleepless nights for the rest of a manager's career if they were to try to consider them all.

Different risks can be dealt with in different ways. Some, such as fire and weather, can be insured against. Others, such as the threat of war or terrorism, can be avoided or at least minimized during the early stages of the strategy process. Risk assessment professionals can be called upon to advise on how best to deal with these. One piece of advice that the professionals give is to only insure against or plan for only those risks which can reasonably be expected to happen. It is theoretically possible that an asteroid could wipe out your head office, but the chance is so remote as to not be worth insuring against (even assuming you could get cover). Meanwhile, there are plenty of more likely risks that need to be dealt with.

The biggest risk of all, of course, is simply that things will not go according to plan, and that at some point in time your strategy will start to come unstuck. In reality, this is not a risk at all; it is a near certainty. No matter how carefully you plan, something will go wrong. You may as well assume this from the beginning; and then if nothing does go wrong, you will be pleasantly surprised.

The late Igor Ansoff developed a model of what he called 'environmental turbulence' ('turbulence' being Clausewitz's idea of 'friction' under another name). Ansoff developed a scale for measuring the business environment according to its potential to affect the business's own strategy. The level of turbulence could be measured on three dimensions: *instability* (how frequently events would occur which could affect the business); *discontinuity* (how radical these events would be and whether they would greatly change the environment) and *unpredictability* (how quickly these events would happen and whether they could be predicted). Using this or some other method to look at potential risks and plan for how they will be dealt with should they arise is an essential part of strategy development.

COMMUNICATING THE PLANS
传达计划

Once the strategy has been drawn up and the plans completed, these need to be communicated to all members of the company. This has two purposes: (1) it ensures that everyone knows what their own role is and what is expected of them, and (2) it helps to ensure that employees are committed to making the strategy work and will not try to hinder or impede it. Other groups may also need to be informed. Major shareholders will want to know what the strategy is, in outline form if not in detail, as it is their money which will be lost if things go badly wrong.

IMPLEMENTING THE PLANS
实施计划

The plan is then put into effect, and employees, teams and departments proceed towards their individual goals.

EVALUATING PROGRESS　评估进展

It is vitally important that actual progress should be checked against the plan at regular stages, or continually if possible. Significant gaps appearing between plan and reality is often the first sign that something is going wrong; either the plan was flawed or some unforeseen event has thrown it off course.

ONE STRATEGY OR MANY?
一元战略或多元战略

Much of the foregoing assumes that we are discussing overall strategy affecting the entire business, and that strategy is made at the topmost level of the business. But strategy is, or can be, made and implemented at many different levels of the business. Each department or business unit is likely to have its own strategy, which relates to or forms part of the overall business strategy but is formed and implemented quite outside the boardroom at head office.

Strategy should not be thought of as a monolith. A better

analogy is that of Russian *matroushka* dolls. You may well have seen these in souvenir shops: a painted wooden figure of a doll is lifted up to reveal another, slightly smaller doll inside, which in return reveals yet another even smaller doll, and so on. A fully developed business strategy in fact consists of a whole series of strategies that interlock and nest into each other, all fitting together like parts of a puzzle.

Most critically, the various functional departments of a business will each have their own strategies for carrying out their particular work. Here are some examples:

- *Marketing strategy*—this type of strategy considers how best to market goods and services to customers. It includes considerations such as what products to make, what price to charge, how best to advertise, and also which customers to target (see Chapter 5).

- *Human resources strategy*—this type of strategy focuses on how many employees the company requires and what their capabilities and skills should be. Recruitment of new employees, retention of existing employees, and how to provide training and to enable these employees to develop and expand their abilities are all part of the strategy (see Chapter 4).

- *Technology strategy*—technology requires investment, and so the company needs a strategy for technology development. What new technologies are coming along, and which ones should the company adopt?

- *Financial strategy*—given the ever-increasing complexity of international financial markets, it is more important than ever for a company to have a strategy for managing its financial assets, its debts and its relationship with shareholders (see Chapter 7).

These are just some of the specific strategies that exist within the general framework: there are many others.

WHOSE JOB IS STRATEGY?
谁负责战略决策

One of the questions that has perplexed academics and writers on strategy in recent years is the question of who 'does' strategy. Who is responsible for defining goals, assessing options and deciding what the strategy should be?

Because business strategy was originally a straight transfer from the principles of military strategy, it followed that business strategy used to be set according to the command-and-control principles used by the military. In the army, it is the general who determines strategy; therefore in business it should be the managing director, or at least the board, who determines strategy. Goals were set at the top of the organization, and responsibility for meeting them was passed down the line. After a time, business leaders noted that generals devolved much responsibility for planning to members of their staff (most armies have a planning section as part of their general staff, which does nothing else except generate plans and strategies), and so big companies that could afford to set up their own strategy and planning departments.

The last two decades have seen this begin to change. First, the command-and-control approach to management has fallen out of favour (we will discuss this in more detail later in the book), and the emphasis today—nominally, at least—is on decentralization and democratization. The argument goes that it is better to give people responsibility for setting their own strategies, on the grounds that (a) they know best what their own capabilities are, and (b) they are more likely to commit to making the strategy work if it is their own idea, rather than something foisted on them without consultation from above. The role of head office then retreats to being one of establishing overall goals and a very general strategic framework within which each business unit or department operates, and then allowing the latter to get on with it. This can be very successful; the German media and publishing group Bertelsmann grew to be the third largest such company in the world using a very decentralized framework within which individual businesses were given very general financial targets and allowed to make up their own mind how they reached them.

Japanese companies also do things slightly differently. Ohmae Kenichi, in his book *The Mind of the Strategist* (1982), described how strategy in successful Japanese companies emerges out of discussions and debates within the company generally. The strategy makers, whom Ohmae calls the *samurai*, are often not senior managers at all, but talented junior managers who are able to bring fresh perspectives to the business and its needs. Senior management's role is to guide the process and allow a consensus to emerge across the company as to what the strategic priorities and objectives should be.

An even more radical model has emerged in Brazil. An experiment in decentralization at a manufacturing company called Semco took on a life of its own, and has now reached the point where, according to the chairman, Ricardo Semler, top management has no responsibility for strategy at all. Everyone in the company understands what needs to be done to help the company grow, and they simply consult with each other as necessary and get on and do it. Senhor Semler freely admits that his own job is now almost entirely redundant.

Not everyone can cope with ideas this radical. In fact, most companies prefer a compromise between command-and-control and full decentralization. Primary responsibility for overall strategy rests still with top management, and the board of directors remains the body with ultimate authority over strategic matters. But many more detailed aspects of strategy are handed down to the teams or departments responsible for them. And well-managed companies try, at least, to solicit opinions from employees about what strategies the company might adopt and what impacts these strategies might have on themselves, the employees. This is particularly the case when the strategy being considered might result in job losses.

Another theory, which has been spelled out in some detail by the former Cambridge academic John Child, holds that strategy is ultimately made by those who have access to power. Those managers who have the most influence within the company are able to influence and control strategic decisions. Again these managers are not necessarily those in the most senior positions. An example of this comes from the steel-maker Corus in early 2003. Corus had been formed a few years earlier through the merger of a large British company and a smaller French one. In 2003, the board of Corus announced it wished to sell one division of the company in order to pay off some of its debts. This decision was contested within the company by managers based in the Netherlands. Although they were in a minority within the company, the division they controlled was also the most profitable part of the company, and they knew they had power. They objected to the sale, and eventually took legal action against Corus—their own company—to stop it going through. Thus this minority were able reshape the company's business strategy to suit their own view.

HOW MANAGERS DO STRATEGY
管理者如何制定战略

Much of the literature on strategy makes a fundamental assumption that strategy-making is a rational process. Managers take strategic decisions based on full knowledge of their own business and its environment. Those decisions are made rationally by considering the evidence and working out the best possible solution.

Studies of managers in action, however, have cast doubt

on whether strategy is actually done this way. In a series of articles in *Harvard Business Review* in the 1970s and in a later series of books, the Canadian academic Henry Mintzberg suggested that most managers actually spend very little of their time engaged in formal planning and strategy-making. The day-to-day pressures of work mean that managers are constantly having to respond to events and people around them. Decisions are often required quickly, before there is time to collect all the facts and analyze them in detail. Opportunities have to be grasped before they disappear. In these situations, strategy tends to be made 'on the wing', with decisions taken more or less intuitively based on the information that is immediately available. Mintzberg believes that very few managers actually make strategy in a formal and rational way. Instead, strategy 'emerges' in an informal and *ad hoc* way as a result of a series of decisions that are taken in various parts of the organization.

Time is an important constraint on how managers create and develop strategies, and this is true at many levels of the organization. As Mintzberg suggests, many managers have to settle for second best; instead of arriving at carefully considered decisions, they 'muddle though' and hope that a combination of background knowledge and intuition will help them make the right decision. The idea that managers exist in a less than rationally perfect world had been noted earlier by the American psychologist and cyberneticist Herbert Simon, who coined the term 'satisficing' to indicate a result that, while less than perfect, is good enough to meet ordinary needs. Most managers, it is argued, look for decisions and outcomes that will 'satisfice' rather than yield the best possible result. The idea of 'muddling through' comes from another American scholar, Charles Lindblom, who suggested that most managers and administrators make decisions based on irrational as well as rational factors. The work of Mintzberg and other recent writers suggests that little has changed since Lindblom's day.

Nor is the idea that strategy should 'emerge' or evolve from out of the business rather than being defined and imposed from the top down necessarily a bad one. Indeed, that is how decisions are made in many organizations. Before becoming a management consultant with the US-based firm McKinsey & Co. , Ohmae Kenichi had trained as both a nuclear physicist and a classical musician. In both nuclear power plants and symphony orchestras, a certain amount of collective learning and decision-making is essential if they are to function smoothly. People share knowledge and ideas naturally, and decisions are formed from these interactions. Ohmae believes that businesses can do this as well, and, as noted above, shows how many Japanese businesses already do make strategy in this way. But Ohmae believes such a way of making strategy is foreign to the mindset of most American and European managers. Without going into his argument in detail, he believes that cultural differences, especially in areas such as the production and codification of knowledge (see Chapter 8) mean that Western managers do not see strategy as integral to the business. Rather, they see it as just another 'activity' to be carried out.

So we have three ideas about how strategy is done:
- formally and rationally, as a separate activity, what might be called 'planned strategy';
- *ad hoc* and on an ongoing basis, what Mintzberg calls 'emergent strategy';
- evolving out of discussions and interactions, what Ohmae calls 'evolved strategy' .

All three have their advantages and disadvantages, and there is some truth to Ohmae's view that cultural differences influence the ways strategy is made. Nevertheless some American companies, notably Intel and, to a lesser extent, Microsoft conduct at least some of their strategic thinking and decision-making in an evolutionary way, seeking input and ideas from all parts of the company and arriving at decisions by consensus. And interestingly, a century ago the British chocolate makers Cadbury used a variety of methods including suggestions schemes, consultations and strategic review by works committees to formulate strategies through consensus (it is worth noting that Cadbury rose to be the world's largest maker of confectionery during this period).

How managers make strategy will always be subject to many variables: time and other strategic constraints, cultural background and, importantly, the ability of the managers themselves to think creatively about strategy. In a nicely circular process, one of the key core competencies that managers must consider when making strategy is their own competency to make strategy!

IMPLEMENTATION　实施战略

The Prussian military theorist Karl von Clausewitz was one of those who believed that the best strategies are the simplest because they are most flexible and easy to adapt to changing circumstances or 'friction'. But, he famously commented, 'Everything in strategy is very simple, but that does not mean that everything in strategy is very easy.'

Implementing a strategy is one of the hardest things of all. It is rare for *any* strategy to be completely successful and to be implemented exactly as it was planned. The best and most carefully thought out and analyzed strategy can still fail, with costly results for all concerned. Every day in the financial press we read of mergers that have gone wrong, once powerful companies that are on the verge of failing, products which took years and cost millions to develop that have had to be abandoned because no one wants to buy them. It is easy to assume that the managers who made these decisions in the first place were incompetent or foolish. In fact, more importantly—and more worryingly— many of these decisions were made by managers who were very competent and very knowledgeable indeed, and who may well have taken the right decision on the first instance. The strategy was right: but the implementation was all wrong.

What drives strategies off the rails and causes them fail? We referred above to concepts like friction and turbulence, environmental factors that create pressures to deviate from the strategy. New competitors suddenly enter the market unannounced. The government introduces new health and safety regulations and compliance with these pushes costs up. Key employees quit or join a rival company. Customer tastes change and products become suddenly obsolete, sometimes even before they are launched. A natural disaster can happen, or the economy can suddenly experience a downturn. The list of what can go wrong is almost endless.

There are two ways of responding to the threat of turbulence or friction. The first is to try to anticipate those things that are most likely to go wrong, and to develop alternative strategies, known as contingency plans, for dealing with these should they arise. Having a set of contingency plans on hand is a bit like having insurance; you hope you will never need them, but if you do, they are there and ready to be put into action, saving valuable time.

The second is to ensure that plans are reasonably flexible and can be adapted or changed in the light of new circumstances. If, for example, a new competitor emerges on the scene halfway through the implementation of a strategy, and even if this had not been predicted or foreseen, the strategy should be flexible enough to allow the business to respond without losing sight of its original goal and objectives. This brings us back to the idea of simplicity; in general, simple strategies are more flexible than complex ones.

Many strategies fail, though, for reasons that have nothing to do with the environment. Internal problems caused by lack of communication, misunderstanding, confusion and even outright resistance to the strategy by employees are major potential problems.

Simple misunderstandings and confusion over who is supposed to do what can usually be avoided through good communications. It is always important to communicate a strategy clearly, from the outset, to all employees—even those who may not necessarily be directly involved in its implementation. Everyone's tasks and responsibilities need to be spelled out, as do the potential impacts of the strategy on them personally (will they have to do more work, will they be paid more, are their jobs under threat, etc.).

More serious is the problem that can arise when employees and managers deliberately set out to impede or wreck a strategy. An extreme case is that of Corus, described above, when a virtual civil war broke out inside the company. More commonly, individual employees or groups of employees turn to what the American sociologist and management scholar Chris Argyris calls 'defensive routines'. Argyris believes that most employees in most organizations are strongly resistant to change, for a whole variety of reasons. They may feel that the change threatens them personally (and sometimes, of course, they are right); they may simply dislike change of any sort and react automatically when change is threatened. Sometimes employees and managers believe that proposed changes are wrong and will damage an organization, and feel it is their duty as loyal employees to prevent these from going through. For whatever reason, many employees will resist change—and as nearly all strategies require at least some change for some people, their resistance can hinder implementation or even stop it in its tracks.

What can be done about this? Again, the key is communication: making sure everyone is clear about the nature of the changes and the benefits the new strategy will bring should eliminate the mistaken resistance from those who believe they are acting in the company's best interests. Care needs to be given to how other potential resistance can be dealt with, through incentives, sanctions, or a combination of the two. At all events, no strategy should proceed to implementation unless and until the managers responsible for that strategy are sure that everyone else in the company is ready and willing to carry it out. To borrow another adage from the military, 'never give an order unless you are sure it will be obeyed'.

STRATEGY AND STRUCTURE
战略与结构

There is a very strong link between strategy and organization. All organizations need a strategy to tell them where to go and how to get there, while all strategies need an organization capable of implementing them and making them work. The exact nature of the relationship is still being debated by theorists. The American business historian Alfred Chandler, generally regarded as the founder of modern business strategy, coined the phrase 'structure follows strategy', indicating the subordination of the former: a business should first define its strategy, then build or adapt its organization so as to implement that strategy. In the 1990s, though, two other American writers, James Collins and Jerry Porras, argued that there were many cases of successful businesses which had first established an organization and only then developed a strategy. The electronics firms Hewlett Packard and Sony are two examples of businesses where a team of people came together without at first any clear idea of what they wanted to make and sell, and only gradually evolved a strategy to suit them.

A good concept to remember here is 'organizational fitness for purpose', which comes from two American academics writing in the late 1970s, Raymond Miles and Charles Snow. This means simply that there must be a match between, on the one hand, the abilities and resources of the business, and on the other hand, the goals the business has set for itself. Which comes first, strategy or structure, does not matter so long as this basic fit is maintained and achieved. This needs to borne in mind as we move on to the next chapter, which discusses organizations in more detail.

摘要

● 每个企业都需要一个战略，以指导其运作的重点并帮助它实现自己的目标。

● 制定战略有许多方式和方法，但是最终都涉及分析企业当前的地位和环境，定义和评估目标和战略选择，选择适合情况的最好的选择方案，然后实施选定的战略。

● 理想情况下，战略可以用理性的方式制定，但是总是存在一些阻止管理人员按照理想的方式制定战略的限制。在实践中，制定战略有很多有创造性的和主观的因素。

● 实施是战略最难的部分，因为在企业自身内部和企业环境里存在许多风险和问题。

● 最后，战略成功与否至少部分依赖于执行战略的组织，组织和战略的匹配至关重要。

SUGGESTIONS FOR FURTHER READING
延伸阅读

Ansoff, I., *Corporate Strategy*, New York: John Wiley & Sons, 1965. *Dated but still influential; Ansoff was one of the first thinkers after Chandler (below) to look at theories of business strategy. He was particularly interested in the relationship between the strategies of individual businesses and the environments in which they operate. His Strategic Management (New York: John Wiley & Sons, 1979) is an updating of his earlier work.*

Chandler, A. D., *Strategy and Structure: Chapters in the History of the American Industrial Enterprise*, Cambridge, MA: MIT Press, 1962.

Often regarded as the founding text of modern business strat-

egy, this is an excellent and eminently readable book which ex-amines the relationship between strategy and organization, using historical case studies.

Collins, J. and Porras, J. , *Built to Last: Successful Habits of Visionary Companies*, New York: Harper Business, 1994.

Excellent and readable, showing how successful businesses think about strategy and goals, and how to reach them.

Hamel, G. and Prahalad, C. K. , *Competing for the Future: Breakthrough Strategies*, Boston, MA: Harvard Business School Press, 1989.

This work introduced the idea of core competencies and of fo-cusing strategy on customers, not on the environment as previous formal strategy had suggested. The book has its critics, but con-tains much food for thought.

Mintzberg, H. , *The Rise and Fall of Strategic Planning*, New York: Free Press, 1993.

This is Mintzberg's principal critique of formal strategy; he also comments on similar themes in Mintzberg on Management (*New York: Free Press*, 1989).

Ohmae, K. , *The Mind of the Strategist*, New York: McGraw-Hill, 1982.

This book remains very popular and has been continuously in print for over twenty years. Although Ohmae sets out to explain how Japanese companies and managers think about strategy, he has much to say on the subject to all managers everywhere.

Porter, M. , *Competitive Strategy: Techniques for Analyzing Industries and Competitors*, New York: The Free Press, 1980.

An influential if often criticized work on formal strategy; see also his Competitive Advantage: Creating and Sustaining Superi-or Performance (*New York: The Free Press*, 1985). *Both can be technical for the non-specialist.*

3

ORGANIZATION

组　　　织

Structure arises as soon as people begin to do something together.

（Thomas North Whitehead）

组织结构产生于人类开始集体做事。

——托马斯·诺斯·怀特黑德

In Chapter 1 we spoke of business in terms of three core concepts: *purpose, structure and function*. Chapter 2 showed how the purpose and goals of a business can be defined and set, and how strategy is made. In this chapter we move on to the second core concept, structure. In order to achieve its aims and purposes, a business has to bring together a series of elements—people, resources, technology and so on—and combine them so that they work effectively together. This in turn requires an organization.

Creating and sustaining an organization is one of the most important aspects of management. Indeed, some theorists regard organization as the single most important aspect of management. It is hard to overstate the importance of organization, for without a properly functioning organization a business cannot reasonably expect to meet its goals.

Organization is a very complex field, both in theory and in practice. Organizations tend to be unique, making it difficult if not impossible to generalize about them. They also tend to change and evolve, so that a theory that appears to be correct at one moment becomes outdated the next. In particular organizations are (usually) constantly growing, creating sub-organizations within themselves and spinning off new organizations which they then control. In order to keep matters simple, we will here consider organizations of a fairly simple form, and will look at single organizations only; we will not, for example, look at cases of businesses owned by other businesses such as conglomerates or holding companies (the role that these play will be discussed briefly in Chapter 7). In reading this basic account of what organizations are and what they do, the reader needs to be aware that the real picture can be much more complex.

DEFINITIONS 定义

As said, the study of organizations is a very complex field, and a considerable vocabulary of terms and jargon has built up over the years. The following terms will be commonly encountered:

Organization theory   Organization theory is a body of 组织理论
management theory that studies how organizations are constructed, comparing different types and how they perform in different circumstances. Some organization theorists study organizations as they actually exist, while others look for an ideal type of organization. Organization theory shows how business organizations have changed and evolved over the years, and will continue to do so in the future.

Organization behaviour   Rather confusingly, this term 组织行为
has two meanings. It is most commonly used in a broad sense to mean the whole field of the study of organizations, including organization theory (above). Originally, though, it referred to the specific study of how organizations function. Drawing heavily on fields such as psychology, sociology and political science, among others, as well as on specific studies of business organi-

zations in a variety of settings, organization behaviour seeks to unravel the complex relationships that exist within and between organizations, and to understand how they can be better managed, created and changed.

结构

Structure　The structure of an organization refers to how the organization is built and the relationship of its constituent parts to each other. Bureaucracies, line and staff organizations, network organizations and virtual organizations are all examples of structures; we will turn to these and other examples in more detail below.

层级制度

Hierarchy　Closely related to structure, hierarchy determines the organizational 'pecking order'. In theory, by knowing their place in the hierarchy, each member of the organization knows their own responsibilities, who they report to and who reports to them, and what level of authority they have. Hierarchies are often described as having 'layers', with the top layers being senior management and the board of directors, the bottom layers being shop-floor workers or their equivalent, and other layers of 'middle management' in between. More recent theories of organization tend to regard hierarchy as being at best a necessary evil, and stress the importance of democracy and equality within the organization. However, at least some hierarchy is present in almost every business organization.

沟通

Communication　Communication is essential within organizations as it allows knowledge to be circulated, and without knowledge organizations cannot function (see Chapter 8). Communication is sometimes spoken of as being either vertical—between layers of the hierarchy—or horizontal—between different departments or business units at the same level within the hierarchy. Communication can take a variety of forms: formal memos and letters, e-mails, formal meetings, or private and casual conversations.

协调

Co-ordination　Sometimes also known as control (though this term is becoming outdated in many circles), co-ordination is what managers do in order to bring all the elements of the organization together and make sure they are pulling in the same direction. An organization which is badly co-ordinated features individuals and groups working without reference to each other, often wasting effort, sometimes working at cross-purposes. In a well-co-ordinated organization, everyone is aware of what everyone else is doing and is working in harmony towards the same goal. It goes without saying that good communications are vital to co-ordination. Achieving co-ordination is one of the most important and difficult tasks of the manager.

Departments/business units　　Departments and business units are smaller 'organizations within an organization'. They come into existence when the business becomes too large to be co-ordinated and managed from a single point, or when specialist functions need to be added. Departments are usually dedicated to a single function, such as marketing, human resource management, finance, purchasing, etc., while business units are usually self-contained mini-businesses with people from various functions working together. Business units may be established when expanding to another location (a company based in Chicago might set up a separate business unit to handle business in New York), or to focus on new and different products and services (a sporting goods manufacturer might have one business unit making skis and another making golf clubs). Departments are usually integrated into the company, while business units may have a degree of autonomy; indeed larger business units will often have their own small functional departments, as above.

部门

Groups and teams　　Groups and teams are the smallest sub-units of the organization. They are usually assembled to perform particular tasks, and can be composed of managers and workers of different grades, from upper management to the shopfloor. The two terms are often used interchangeably, but in general teams are formally constituted and usually have an offi-

群体和团队

cial leader, either chosen by team members or appointed from outside. Sizes can vary, but the majority of teams have between four and ten members. Groups are sometimes larger, and often are not formally constituted and have no official leader.

网络组织

Networks　Networks are relationships between people that do not depend on hierarchy. In other words, networks treat all members as equal, and do not regard any one portion of the network as dominant, unlike hierarchy which has a descending scale of ranks and seniority. Networks are often structured from the centre outwards (rather than from the top down, as in hierarchies), rather like a spider's web. More radical forms of network have no organized centre at all and have seemingly random patterns of relationships. Networks are sometimes seen as an alternative to hierarchy, but in fact can co-exist with hierarchy within an organization. That is, an organization that is hierarchically structured can also have networks that enable communication and management.

文化

Culture　Culture consists of the shared beliefs, ideas, traits and even emotions that are held in common by most or all members of the organization. Every organization has its culture, and we will go into this in more detail in Chapter 9. For the moment, what is important about culture is that it affects virtually all other concepts in organization. How people communicate, how they see the hierarchy (if any) and their own role in it, how they respond to and interact with each other in groups and teams, how they work and think are all influenced by culture. The impact of culture is particularly noticeable when it comes to the management of change.

PROBLEMS IN THE STUDY OF ORGANIZATION　组织研究中的问题

Given the importance of organization, it is hardly surprising that there should be many theories about it. Business organizations have been studied using methods and concepts imported from virtually every other discipline, from physics and biology to history and aesthetics. Chaos theory, molecular biology, Darwinian evolution, Marxist dialectics, poetic logic, computer science, neural networks and other theories of human brain activity, science fiction and the teachings of Confucius are just some of the ideas that have been applied in order to understand more fully what organizations are and how they work.

Despite all this activity, there remains much disagreement as to what constitutes an organization, how it should be structured and how it should be managed. No generally agreed total theory of organization exists; there is no organizational equivalent to the theory of relativity, for example. The Welsh-born Canadian scholar Gareth Morgan has argued that this is because organizations are too complex for any single theory to completely capture them. Organizations are multi-faceted: they are made up of an array of human beings and technology working together, often in vastly different ways, and increasingly in quite different places, and they can look quite different depending on which angle you view them from. Any one theory of organization, says Morgan in his book *Images of Organization*, will only illuminate one facet. To really understand organizations properly, we need to use many different kinds of theory and explanation. Some theorists see organizations as machines, structured like mechanical objects; others see them as biological organisms, growing and changing in an evolutionary manner. And it may be, says Morgan, that both these concepts are right, up to a point. Business organizations are both machines and living organisms, and a lot of other things besides.

Two other factors complicate the study of organizations still further. First, no two organizations are identical. Their formal structure might appear to be similar, but there will always be differences, and often these differences will be subtle and hard to detect. Another Canadian theorist, Henry Mintzberg, suggests that organizations evolve and adapt themselves to their environment, and that each takes on a unique character as a result. Others believe that because organizations are made up of people, and people are all individuals, organizations will be individual in nature as well. But for whatever reason, no two organizations are exactly the same, and therefore generalizing about them is very difficult.

Second, as in many areas of management, there is a considerable gap between theory and practice when it come to organizations. A number of 'best' models or ideal types of organization have been created and extensively discussed, but it remains the case that most organizations do not conform to any of these ideals. Most organizations are, in fact, imperfect, and in practical terms much of a manager's time can be spent dealing with these imperfections. Trying to rid the organization of these imperfections and make the organization 'better' leads us to one of the most problematic issues in all of management, the management of change. We will discuss change management later in this chapter, but for now it is important to remember that many theories of organization discuss ideal organizations rather than actual ones. Any consideration of the 'best' form of organization has to include a discussion of how to create it, either by building a new organization from scratch or adapting and changing an existing one.

ORGANIZATION AND STRATEGY
组织与战略

Orthodox thinking for many years held that a company's organization had to be aligned behind its strategy, and that therefore the correct way to do things was first to decide on goals and strategy, and then design an organization that would fit that strategy. This was the conclusion reached by Alfred Chandler in his landmark book *Strategy and Structure*, a study of the development of modern corporations in the first half of the twentieth century. However, alternative views have begun to emerge. In the late 1990s, James Collins and Jerry Porras conducted another study of American firms that have been successful over time, such as Hewlett-Packard. In *Built to Last*, Collins and Porras argued that many great companies first come together as a collection of like-minded individuals who form an organization but have no clear purpose beyond a desire to work together. Decisions such as what strategy to follow and what products to make emerge only slowly.

The findings of Collins and Porras, that structure does not necessarily follow strategy (as Chandler suggested) can be confirmed by looking at other examples around the world. One of the world's most successful electronics firms, Sony, was founded in the immediate aftermath of the Second World War by a group of Japanese entrepreneurs, including Ibuka Masaru and Morita Akio. These entrepreneurs, working out of a single office in one of the few buildings still standing in bombed-out Tokyo, had little idea of what markets there were or what resources they could call on. They did, however, have a pool of talent to draw upon and believed that they could be successful. Again, decisions on strategy and core product areas emerged only slowly. Sony's basic strategy has also changed a number of times down through the years, but its organization has remained fundamentally the same.

Rather than a rigid doctrine that structure must follow strategy or vice versa, the American scholars Raymond Miles and Charles Snow suggest the concept of ' organizational fitness for purpose' . What this phrase means is that as close a match as possible must be made between the organization, its capabilities and its resources on the one hand, and the goals the organization is trying to achieve on the other. An organization that cannot achieve its purpose will, by definition, fail. This seems obvious: but many businesses fail quite simply because they are not fit for purpose and cannot achieve their goals. Other businesses fail when goals and strategies change, but it then proves impossible to make the necessary changes in the organization.

THE COMPONENTS OF ORGANIZATION 组织的组成部分

Bearing in mind that, as noted above, every organization is unique, each will be built up and structured in different ways. However, there are some common elements that all business organizations will have.

Every organization is made up of a variety of smaller units, including business units, departments, groups and teams as described above, and finally the smallest unit of all, the individual worker or manager. How many of these units and what exactly they do will depend on the size of the organization, the nature of the business it does, and where it is located. It is almost impossible to generalize about organizations in this way. Some very large businesses (steel mills for example) have just a single physical site where tens of thousands of people are employed; others, such as airlines, may employ comparatively few people, but those people may be dispersed in small offices or business units around the country or around the world.

How these units are organized and structured depends, as we say, on the nature of the business. Figure 3. 1 shows three examples of different types of business: a consultancy business, an airline and an automobile manufacturer. You will see that there are three quite different configurations, each of which has been designed to help the company meet its strategic targets and goals. Some elements are common: for example, all three have marketing departments and all three have accounting departments. But some elements are unique to the organization in question. Here we see the concept of 'organizational fitness for purpose' coming into play again: organizations adapt themselves and configure themselves according to the industry they are in and their environment.

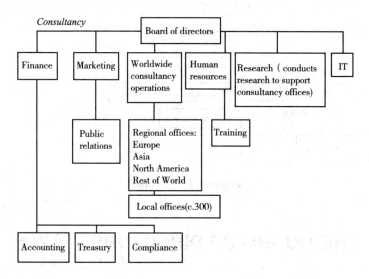

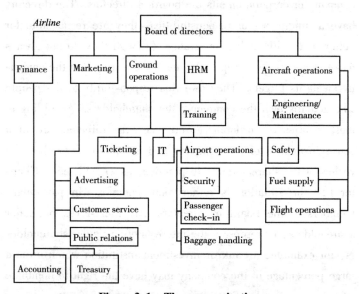

Figure 3.1   Three organizations

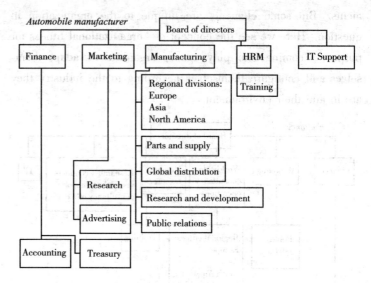

Figure 3. 1　continued

THE BOARD OF DIRECTORS　董事会

At the top of the organizational hierarchy in any limited company or corporation sits the board of directors. The directors have a unique set of responsibilities: they are responsible for policy and, ultimately, for strategy (though they do not always make strategy; see Chapter 2) and for ensuring that the company meets its targets. They owe this responsibility to the people who actually own the company, the shareholders. According to most theories of corporate governance, the directors are in a sense custodians of the company and are required to obey the wishes of the shareholders. In practice, as we will see in Chapter 12, the situation is rather more complex. In particular, members of the board of directors may themselves be major shareholders, or represent the interests of particular shareholders: for example, a bank or investment institution which owns a large percentage of the company may have the right to nominate one or more people of its choice to the board of directors.

Boards of directors are required by law in nearly every jurisdiction around the world for any registered company. The board must have a chairman, and usually at least three other directors. Typical boards of directors are composed of a chairman, a managing director or chief executive officer, and a number of what are known as executive directors, each of which is responsible for a particular aspect of the business. Thus a finance director or chief financial officer may be in charge of corporate finance, a marketing director will be in charge of marketing, and so on. Directors were once commonly known as vice-presidents, thus the vice-president for marketing, vice-president for finance and so on, but this term is now less common; it is now used mainly in American companies, and often connotes a manager at a level below that of the board.

In addition, most boards have a number of non-executive directors, who have no day-to-day function within the company but act as advisers to the rest of the board. Sometimes these are nominated by major shareholders, at other times they are nominated by the board itself. Non-executive directors are required to be people of experience and integrity, who can comment effectively on proposed strategies and policies. They also conduct some external functions such as auditing accounts, determining pay and compensation packages for senior managers, and recruiting new executive directors when necessary.

Probably the most important relationship within the board is that between the chairman and the managing director/chief executive officer. The chairman conducts board meetings and acts as a kind of co-ordinator for the board itself. He or she is usually also the public face of the company, and often takes prime responsibility for areas such as public relations and relationships with shareholders. The managing director focuses more on the company itself, and is responsible for all aspects of management (in some large companies, responsibility for day-to-day operations may be devolved to a chief operating officer—also a board member—leaving the managing director free to concentrate on broader issues). The chairman and the managing director thus work very closely together, and it is essential that they be able to get along. When the managing director and the chairman are in dispute, the result is often a kind of organizational paralysis, with no one—shareholders and employees included—certain of who is in charge.

It is not a legal requirement that a board have different people filling these posts, and it is not uncommon for the same person to be both chairman and managing director; but the workload in these cases is enormous, and few have the stamina to do this for long.

ORGANIZATIONAL SUB-DIVISIONS
组织的子部门

Small, newly founded businesses often have just a single group of people working together, taking on tasks in an *ad hoc* manner, everyone working together to get the job done. As soon as the business expands past a certain point, however, it becomes necessary to start sub-dividing the organization. Early organization theorists spoke of something called the 'span of control', meaning that once an organization becomes too large, either in terms of numbers of people or geographical dispersion, it becomes more and more difficult to manage. Today, internet technology and e-mail have greatly increased the span of control, and managers can now co-ordinate larger groups of people over greater distances. Nonetheless, limits still exist, and a degree of sub-division is inevitable if the organization is to grow.

The first sub-division is usually the setting up of departments to handle separate functions. A manufacturing company will have a production department responsible for actual manufacturing, and then a variety of departments that handle finance, accounting, human resources, marketing, purchasing, research and development, and so on. A company engaged in providing services (retailing, banking, catering, etc.) will have a front-line service department, again with various supporting departments as above. The next type of sub-division is the business unit. These typically are established to take advantage of a particular market (such as a particular geographical region or a specific group of consumers) or develop a specific group of products or services outside the company's main field of activity. Note that the consultancy firm in Figure 3. 1 has several business units, while the airline has none.

Figure 3. 1 shows some of the ways in which organizations can be sub-divided according to need. Note that the sizes of these subdivisions can be quite unequal. For example, the automobile manufacturer's purchasing department is much smaller than its manufacturing department in terms of numbers of managers and workers employed. And sizes of comparable departments will also vary between organizations: this consultancy firm's marketing department is comparatively small, as most customer contact is handled by consultants themselves, while that of the airline is very large.

It should be noted that many different names for these departments and business units exist. Production departments, for example, can be known as manufacturing departments, engineering departments or any other name the company feels best describes the department and suits its own purpose. Departments, especially large ones, are sometimes also called divisions. Business units too may be known as divisions or reporting units, again according to the tastes of the company and the directors.

Departments and business units will have their own hierarchies. At the top of each is a senior management team who report directly to the board; one member of this team is also often a member of the board (such as the marketing director, finance director, etc.). Below the senior management team are other managers, usually known as 'middle managers', who run smaller teams, groups and work units, and they are assisted by junior managers who work with smaller units still. Finally we come to the employees at the bottom of the hierarchy, including clerks, service staff, salespeople, production line workers and so on. There was formerly a very strong distinction between managers and employees, with terms like 'white-collar workers' and 'blue-collar workers' showing how differently the two groups worked and behaved. Today that distinction is becoming much more blurred, as will be discussed in Chapter 4.

FRONT LINE AND SUPPORT
一线部门和支援部门

Another commonly made distinction within organizations is between 'front line' and 'support' units. The front-line units are those directly engaged in making and/or delivering products and services to customers. In services the front line is sometimes known as the 'front office'; in hotels and catering the term 'front of house' is also used, and there may be other variations elsewhere. Support or 'back office' staff have little or no direct contact with customers or products and services, but provide necessary functions to keep the business going. Human resource management, accounts and financial controls are examples of obvious back office departments.

The position of other departments such as marketing and purchasing can be more ambivalent. Purchasing works with suppliers, and their activities are critical in ensuring that the production departments have the resources they need. Are they in the front line, or do they merely support production? Marketing has within it a number of different sub-functions such as marketing research and planning, and people engaged in these activities are not in contact with customers; but other members of the marketing department such as salespeople and service teams, are in contact. Is the marketing department in the front office or the back office? The answer is a little of both.

THE VALUE CHAIN　价值链

This ambivalence has led some writers to argue that the whole concept of front line and support departments should be abandoned, and that we should instead concentrate on how each department, team and individual fits into the *value chain*. The value chain is a concept that comes from thinking about strategy, and is usually credited to the Harvard academic Michael Porter, who popularized the concept in the late 1980s.

The value chain idea suggests that products pass through a series of stages within the company, beginning as purchased raw materials and ending as a finished product delivered to the customer. At each stage, value is added to the product. For example, when manufacturing cars, production departments first build the basic car and engine, and then add features that make the car more desirable—i. e. , more valuable—in the eyes of the customer. Advanced braking systems, air bags, comfortable seats, CD players, catalytic converters are all features that add value to the basic car.

从价值链的角度来考察组织。

It was once assumed that only the production department created value, but if we look around the company we see that all departments add value, often in obscure ways. The distribution department adds value by ensuring that cars are delivered quickly and reliably to dealers and thus to customers. The purchasing department adds value by sourcing high-quality components, and/or by reducing costs, meaning that the car can be delivered to the customer at a lower price. The marketing department adds value by making customers aware of features they might not be aware of, and by providing after-sales service. The human resources department adds value by ensuring that employees are happy and highly skilled, thus contributing to the quality of the product. Even the finance department contributes by ensuring that the company's finances are well-managed and that resources are available when needed to allow the other departments to carry out their functions.

Using the value chain to see how departments work together (or at least should work together) can be quite valuable, but some distinction between front office and back office is likely to remain. Those departments and teams with direct contact with the customer often require different resources and different skills than those working in the back office. The task for management becomes one of recognizing all these differences while at the same time ensuring that the different units and parts of the organization work together towards the same set of goals.

INDIVIDUALS AND TECHNOLOGY
个人和技术

The smallest unit of the organization is of course the individual, man or woman, worker or manager. Each individual is typically part of a team or group, and that team or group is in turn part of a department, division or business unit. Thus a hierarchical chain is formed extending from the board of directors to the shop floor and to all the support functions of the business.

Organizations are often described in terms of their being collections of individuals. In fact, there is another vital element to organizations as well: the tools and technology with which people do their work. Virtually all work requires technology of some sort, be it as simple as a hammer and saw or as complex as a satellite communications system. It is the interaction between people and technology that makes work possible. We ought, therefore, to properly think of organizations as collections of individuals working with technology.

The synergy between people and technology is thus greater than the sum of the parts. People without tools can do very little, tools without people are inert artefacts. In the same way, the individuals within the organization create a different synergy simply by working together. Studies have shown repeatedly that five people working together in a team will be more effective, by whatever measure, than five people working individually without contact with each other. The same is true on a larger scale across the organization as a whole. Organizations allow labour, knowledge and resources to be shared and made more efficient and more effective than they would be if used by one person working on their own. This realization that organizations as a whole are greater than the sum of their parts has given rise to the concept of organizational capital.

ORGANIZATIONAL CAPITAL
组织资本

Traditionally, the resources of a firm were said to consist of three physical assets: land, labour and capital (meaning finance or money). Since the late nineteenth century, though, economists have realized that businesses also have another, much more intangible form of asset, namely the knowledge and skills of the people they employ. Later economists, notably the late Edith Penrose in the 1950s and 1960s, developed this idea still further, and organizational capital has now become a widely used term.

Organizational capital refers to knowledge, experience, systems, procedures, ways of doing things, understanding of the market and the business environment and a whole host of other intangible factors. It also includes what might be de-

组织资本是指知识、经验、制度、程序、做事情的方式、对市场和企业环境的理解以及一系列其他的无形因素。

scribed as the intangible assets a business possesses: assets that cannot be physically touched and which may be difficult to measure and value, but which nonetheless exist and are important. The oldest and most widely recognized asset of this type is goodwill, the reputation that a business has with its customers and suppliers. Goodwill with customers, for example, means that people are more willing to buy the company's products and services, and this should translate into higher sales and thus higher profits. Related to goodwill is brand equity, the value that a company's brands are said to have in the eyes of consumers (see also Chapter 5). Finally there is intellectual property, an umbrella term relating to copyrights, patents, trademarks and so on. Intellectual property represents ideas that the company has created, which are of value to customers, and which are unique in the marketplace.

We noted above that an organization is greater than the sum of its parts. That difference—between the sum of the parts and the whole—is the organizational capital. It represents things that the organization does and knows and owns collectively, not just as a group of members. Although organizational capital is very hard to value and measure, its importance in competitive terms cannot be overstated. A football team whose members have played together for many years and have a shared set of plays, routines and signals, plus a part-intuitive knowledge of each other and how they perform on the pitch, will nearly always defeat a team whose members have never played together before, even if the second team's players are individually more skilful. In just the same way, a company that works together well and has a strong body of organizational capital will usually be more successful than one that is no more than a collection of individuals working to their own tune, no matter how skilled and trained those individuals are.

THE BEHAVIOUR OF ORGANIZA-TIONS　组织行为

Because organizations are composed of human beings, they are not static. One of the first principles of organization is that they are dynamic things, composed of unique individuals working together. Understanding the relationships between those individuals and how these progress over time is essential to understanding how organizations function. In this understanding we must look at both the individual and the collective, the person and the organization. Further, not everything that happens in organizations is rational and visible; indeed, it has sometimes been argued that organizations themselves have a kind of collective subconscious, where people communicate and understand (or misunderstand) each other on an unspoken basis.

INDIVIDUAL MOTIVATION　个人动机

At the level of the lowest building block, the individual working with technology, organizations are affected by the motivations of the people working within them. We shall have more to say about motivation in the workplace in Chapter 4, but for now, let us simply state that everyone who comes to work does so for a reason: to earn money, to practise a skill, to have companionship and society, and so on. Many people of course come to work for more than one reason. Depending on their reasons, or combinations of reasons, they may have quite differing attitudes to the organization, their peers and their leaders. They may be highly loyal to the organization and desire to work to make it a better place, or they may think primarily of their own needs and aspirations and feel little or no loyalty. They may enjoy working with their colleagues, or they may actively dislike them. They may trust their leaders, or they may fear them. Every individual will have a slightly different perception of the organization, and this will colour their subsequent actions and behaviours.

GROUPS AND TEAMS　群体和团队

As noted above, every individual belongs to a sub-unit of the organization, and at the lowest level this usually means membership of a group or a team. How effectively this group or team functions depends almost entirely on whether its members are capable of working with each other. If they disagree on fundamental principles, or dislike each other on a personal level, then pulling the efforts of the group/team members together to achieve goals will be very difficult, even impossible. It is not unknown for highly skilled individuals who are capable of great individual effort to be unable to function effectively within a team.

This happens, of course, in arenas other than business. The Australian national cricket team, one of the most successful teams in any sport over the last decade, is notable for its rejection of otherwise highly talented players who cannot work effectively within the team structure, in favour of apparent lesser talents who can do so. The team coach points out that many of these supposed lesser talents blossom within the team structure and within a short time their individual skills show great improvement, thanks to the influence of their colleagues and the team atmosphere.

One of the most fascinating areas of organization behaviour is the study of how people work in groups. It has been observed that individual behaviour often actually changes in the group setting; speech and body language will take on new patterns, people who are vociferous in private will become courteous and deferential to other team members—or vice versa.

An effective group or team is one that is more than the just a collection of individuals. It generates and shares knowledge, within itself and with other groups and teams. It creates an atmosphere where everyone works together towards the same goal, often without overt direction or control. Over time, groups and teams develop a collective behaviour of their own, and may even develop reputations within the rest of the organization.

RELATIONSHIPS WITHIN ORGANIZA-TIONS 组织的内部关系

As should be clear from the foregoing, it is both individuals and the relationships between them that lie at the heart of organization behaviour. Relationships can be either formal, laid down as part of the organization's hierarchy, or informal, between groups and individuals.

Formal relationships are usually ones which deal with reporting, co-ordination and control (of which more below). They are, as said, part of the organization's hierarchy, and at the level of the individual may even be spelled out in that individual's job description. Thus the quality assurance manager will have a formal relationship with the chief production manager, as the latter is his superior; the marketing director will have a formal relationship with the sales manager, as the latter is her junior. Formal relationships do not have to be 'formal' in personal terms; where individuals get along well, they may well wish to treat each other informally, and in most organizations this is encouraged. But the relationship remains formal in the sense that it is required as part of the organization's structure, and if the relationship breaks down, the consequences for the organization could be serious. If the sales manager no longer speaks to the marketing director or fails to pass on vital information, then the marketing director's ability to do her job will be seriously impaired.

Formal relationships also exist between departments, again primarily for the purpose of ensuring reporting and feedback. The marketing department will have relationships, ideally at several levels, with the production department in order to pass back information received from customers. Nearly every department or division will have a relationship with the accounting and finance function in order to ensure requirements for financial control are met (see Chapter 7). Again, these formal relationships are necessary to ensure the flow of information and to make the business work effectively.

Informal relationships are not part of the hierarchy, and are not deliberately created by the organization. Rather, they spring up when people begin to work closely together and identify mutual interests or concerns. Often, though not always, they are accompanied by personal acquaintance or friendship. They may take the form of casual conversations in corridors or at lunch, e-mail exchanges, even meetings outside the workplace. These informal relationships can be very valuable, as they allow people to exchange information and ideas in ways not always possible within the formal hierarchy.

Many organizations place high value on these informal relationships, and see them as primary catalysts for creativity and innovation. Two people discussing a problem over lunch may suddenly have insights which days of research by a formal research team had overlooked, simply because different points of view have been brought to bear. Nonaka Ikujiro and Takeuchi Hirotaka in their book *The Knowledge-Creating Company* describe how many leading Japanese companies rely on this kind of informal contact and communication to generate fresh new ideas. In Japan and the West, organizations will often try to deliberately foster informal relationships by breaking down formal barriers and letting people from different departments work together, setting up e-mail discussion groups, organizing regular events for face-to-face discussions, and so on.

Organizations can encourage informal relationships by creating an atmosphere of tolerance, diversity and trust. Managers need to openly encourage people to come forward with opinions and ideas and to share these, in the knowledge that they will not be disciplined or ridiculed if their ideas are not generally acceptable. But organizations cannot control informal relationships, and in situations where there is distrust or antipathy between parts of the organization—especially between the lower levels of the hierarchy and top management—then informal relationships are often used to build alliances and create alternative power centres.

POWER AND DEPENDENCE
权力和依赖

Not all relationships within an organization are relationships of equals. This is particularly true of formal relationships, which often involve one or more people reporting to someone senior to them in the hierarchy. Departments, divisions and business units may also have unequal relationships depending on size, income and resources, numbers of staff and so on. The guiding ideology of the company may play a role here, too: if the company considers itself to be 'marketing oriented' (see Chapter 5), then the marketing may, even subconsciously, be considered to be the most powerful and important department in the organization.

并非所有组织内的关系都是平等的关系。

But informal relationships can also be unequal. Informal relationships may develop between senior and junior staff members based on mutual need and assistance, but other qualities besides seniority may intervene. Personal access to power and resources, personal charisma and ability to persuade others to see things one's own way all play a role. Groups, whether formally constituted or informally brought together, tend to establish an internal pecking order. Again, how this pecking order develops is outside the control of top management, and the emergence of informal leaders at lower levels cannot always be planned for.

"权力"是采取行动或对他人施加影响力的能力。

'Power' is the ability to take actions or exert influence over others. Within formal hierarchies, managers have power over people who report to them—that is, those below them in the organization. In informal relationships, though, people tend to gather power around them according to their ability to do so, and their desire to do so. The result is that power becomes distributed around the organization in some unpredictable ways. This in turn can have unpredictable results. It can result in people feeling quite literally 'empowered', that is, recognizing that they can take control of their own work and its output, which in turn lends confidence and inspires creativity. But power needs to be exercised with discretion and for the good of the company; if it is not, then major problems can result.

The accounting group Arthur Andersen had for many years provided accounting and auditing services to corporate clients. In the 1970s, as was the prevailing fashion at the time, Arthur Andersen also set up a management consulting division to offer advice to clients on more effective management. As time passed, this management consulting arm grew rapidly, and by the early 1990s, although the accountancy division had far more staff, management consulting was bringing in the majority of the company's revenue. According to the authors of *Inside Arthur Andersen*, the senior managers in management consulting knew that this revenue gave them power, and they began to demand a series of changes in Arthur Andersen and gradually used their influence to dominate the accounting division. The culture of the company began to change, from one of providing services to clients to aggressively pursuing sales. The accountancy division was forced to go along with this, and senior managers were brought in who at times encouraged staff to cut corners to keep clients happy. The result was that Andersen auditors overlooked a massive accounting fraud at the energy company Enron, and when Enron finally collapsed this oversight became public knowledge. This failure, coupled with other similar failures at the same time, effectively destroyed Arthur Andersen (Squires *et al.*).

How was power used in the Andersen case? Initially, it was used by a group of dominant managers to oppose the existing board and shape the company's goals to suit themselves. Ultimately, they went on to take over top management positions, thus the company's goals and those of top management were perforce realigned. Whether these managers then used their power ethically is another matter; what matters for the present discussion is that, by gathering power and operating in groups outside the formal hierarchy of the firm, lower-level managers can block or even change the strategy and policies of the organization.

CONTROL AND CO-ORDINATION 控制和协调

The answer to the abuse of power is control and co-ordination. Early management texts spoke repeatedly of the need for control; there was a belief that top management provided the impetus and the will that drove the organization, and that control needed to be exercised in order to ensure that the rest of the organization fell into line. However, it was recognized that there were limits to what control could achieve. In the 1920s the American political scientist Mary Parker Follett argued that co-ordination was far more likely to be effective than straight control; that is, rather than issuing orders and expecting them to be obeyed, managers and leaders of organizations would do better to create a climate in which people knew what needed to be done and would act without direct orders.

控制和协调可防止滥用权力。

Control seeks to dominate people and tell them what to do; coordination seeks to provide a framework within which people work towards a mutually agreed end. In nearly every case, the latter will always be seen as desirable, and a major portion of the manager's task is to provide and maintain such co-ordination frameworks. But for co-ordination to work, the environment within the organization must be one that encourages people to take responsibility and to act without necessarily waiting for orders. Co-ordination works best when there is a large degree of democracy and staff are willing to think and act independently. If they are not, then there may be no alternative but to accept the need for top-down control until the culture of the organization can be changed.

CULTURE 文化

Chapter 9 of this book is devoted entirely to the issue of culture, but we should note briefly here that the culture of an organization can greatly affect its behaviour. By 'culture', we mean the values, beliefs, attitudes and ways of doing things that are shared by everyone—or at least the great majority of people—in the organization. These common beliefs and values mean that people in an organization will perceive things in one way, while people in another organization will perceive them in quite a different way. This can happen even within different parts of the same organization. It could be argued that, in the case of Arthur Andersen, above, the 'gung-ho' competitiveness of the consulting division was quite different from the culture of impartiality and service that had pervaded the accounting division. The clash of cultures as much as the desire for power helped bring about Andersen's downfall.

Culture can be a powerful positive force, or a powerful negative force. A 'progressive' culture that encourages creativity, innovation and change can be a major factor in keeping a business competitive. On the other hand a 'conservative' culture that values existing routines and ways of doing things and sees change in a negative light can be a major drawback. Changing an existing culture is one of the most problematic and difficult tasks in management, and requires patience and strong leadership.

Culture is also difficult to appreciate because it cannot really be measured. Descriptions of cultures are always subjective, using terms like 'progressive', 'conservative', 'market-oriented', 'innovative' and so on, or often combinations of such terms. Even these terms, though, only give a brief idea of what an organization's culture is like. Those who study culture often do so in ways that even they find hard to define and describe. The Indian academic Sumantra Ghoshal speaks metaphorically of how some companies have a certain 'smell' and it is possible to 'sniff out' the atmosphere in a company soon after first arriving on the premises, and some consultants and business advisers mention the same phenomenon. This technique can be very useful, but it is also almost impossible to measure and record. Culture is one of the great intangibles of organization, yet at the same time it is of paramount importance.

EFFECTIVENESS 效果

Organization behaviour is important because, quite simply, how an organization behaves determines its effectiveness. If the people and groups within the organization work together well, communications are good, innovation and creative ideas are valued and encouraged, change is seen as a positive thing and the atmosphere is generally good, then the organization will in all probability be effective and productive. If the opposite of these things applies, then the organization will almost certainly be suffering from major problems.

LEADERSHIP　领导

All of the above comments point to the fact that leadership is essential to any organization. When any of the above elements—motivation, communication between groups, good relationships, control, culture—is lacking or is out of kilter with the needs of the organization, then it is the leaders who must intervene to rectify the situation. Leaders can help motivate their people; leaders are required to direct cultural change; leaders can provide the stimulus for relationships and co-ordination. Leaders can and should influence the behaviour of organizations, and this in turn influences effectiveness and, ultimately, profitability.

Leaders do not just lead by giving orders. They also serve as an example to other members of the organization. The leader has to be not only committed to the organization, but also to be seen to be committed; if the leader's actions and words do not match, then other members of staff will begin to have doubts. 'Do as I say, not as I do' is never a credible maxim for a leader. 'Follow me and work with me' is more likely to produce the desired effect. A popular metaphor for business leadership is the relationship between an orchestra conductor and his or her players. The conductor does not tell the players what to do; they already know how to play their instruments, possibly better than the conductor does. Instead, the conductor provides a kind of guide and reference point to which the players can look, indicating tempo and changes. Good conductors do not lead the orchestra, they carry it with them.

Finally, the leader has a role to play in planning and stimulating change. They do not necessarily lead change or direct it, but they provide a catalysis, a source of inspiration and motivation for change that gradually spreads throughout the organization. Particularly in the present era, when change is a constant pressure for most organizations, the leader's judgement as to what needs changing and when and his or her subsequent ability to manage that change is one of the most precious things an organization can have.

ORGANIZATIONAL CHANGE　组织变革

　　Much has been said above about change in organizations. Change is an important issue because the environment in which businesses operate is itself constantly changing. Customer needs and tastes change. New technology makes new products, and new methods of production, possible. Competitors make new moves, enter new markets and launch new products that can threaten the competitive position of existing businesses. Governments introduce new laws and regulations. Social pressures require businesses to conform to new expectations concerning ethical behaviour, the natural environment, and so on. And things change inside the organization, too; people come and go, and even for those who stay, needs and motivations change.

　　Some, such as the American consultant Tom Peters, argue that change is a constant: 'the only thing you can be sure of is that everything is changing' is an often heard expression of this view. The argument that change is a continuous process suggests that businesses and management need to be constantly changing as well in order to keep pace. Others see change as a much more uneven phenomenon. Andrew Grove, chairman of semiconductor maker Intel, suggests that there tend to be intervals of stability punctuated by sudden and unexpected change. These times of change, which Grove terms 'strategic inflection points', can neither be predicted nor planned for; all the organization can do is use the times of stability to make sure it is sufficiently strong and flexible to withstand change. Another recent author, Jim Collins, argues in his book *Good to Great* that some things are changing steadily while others are not; for example, technology may be changing all the time, but there are some fundamentals of management that remain constant. One of the arts of management, says Collins, is to know what to change and when to change it, and what to leave alone.

UNPLANNED CHANGE　无计划改变

Change can be divided into two types, unplanned change and planned change. Unplanned change consists of changes in the environment, moves by competitors and regulators, evolving needs of customers and so on that are outside the control of the business. However, organizations themselves change in unplanned ways. Just as people themselves change, their needs and motivations evolving in response to different stimuli, so organizations as a whole will change and evolve as well. Unplanned and unsought, this kind of change can have hard consequences for management.

Example of unplanned change include the loss of key staff members, especially senior managers and leaders, with a consequent loss of impetus and motivation in the organization; the emergence of new and unofficial groups or alliances of employees with their own personal agenda for change (or for resisting change); sudden breakthroughs by research teams, or the emergence of new creative ideas elsewhere in the organization that change ideas and attitudes; sudden unforecast growth in key markets; and so on. The list of possibilities is almost endless. Practising managers are familiar with the phenomenon whereby the organization changes and evolves, steadily and imperceptibly, in response to a variety of internal and external pressures. Very few organizations end up looking like they did when first founded.

PLANNED CHANGE　有计划改变

Planned change, by contrast, is that which is desired and

needed by the organization and its managers, who will deliberately set changes in motion. There is an irony that, while unplanned change happens whether the manager wants it or not and is usually unstoppable, planned change can be very difficult to implement.

Examples of planned change can include the introduction of a new product line, the implementation of a new production technology, the introduction of new financial control and reporting systems, reshaping the organization to change the structure of its departments and divisions or switch to a new organizational type such as the matrix organization or virtual organization (below), increasing the size of the organization by hiring new people, or decreasing the size by making people redundant, changing strategic direction to focus on new goals, and so on. Again, there is virtually no limit to the kinds of changes that can be planned, provided the organization has the resources and capacity to carry them out.

BARRIERS TO CHANGE　变化障碍

Planned changes must of course be costed and prepared for. The resources the business needs, including financial resources, must be available and put in place. Many change programmes fail because they are improperly prepared for. Failure to adequately estimate costs is a common mistake; changes turn out to be more expensive than estimated, and the business suddenly finds it does not have enough money to carry the changes through. Thus changes must be carefully planned; contingency planning (what managers will do if things start to go wrong) is usually also called for.

The most difficult barriers to change, however, often come within the organization. Unless the organization's leaders and other key managers can explain the proposed changes to other staff and persuade them that the changes are in the organization's best interests, there is a risk that staff will resist the changes and try to thwart them. The organization behaviour theorist Chris Argyris describes what he calls 'defensive routines', acts of resistance by staff against changes with which they do not agree. Sometimes staff will be motivated by fear for their personal positions, reluctant to exchange present security for future uncertainty. Sometimes too they will see the proposed changes as threatening to the organization as a whole; believing that they know better than top management what is good for the organization, they will take independent action to thwart the latter. Defensive routines can be as simple as passive resistance, refusing to carry out instructions or pass on information, or more active resistance such as protests, complaints or even industrial action such as strikes.

FORMS OF ORGANIZATION 组织形式

As noted, the elements of organization can be combined in many different ways, and each organization will be unique. Nonetheless, some basic forms of organization are particularly widespread. There is usually, for any given type, an orthodox view of an ideal type of organization, along with other and more radical approaches. In practice, most businesses tend to be hybrids, with elements of more than one ideal type. There follows a brief look at some of the most important and influential ideal types.

CENTRALIZED ORGANIZATIONS
集中组织

The first forms of business organization tended to be very centralized, reflecting perhaps the social conditions of the time. Society in the eighteenth and nineteenth centuries was very authoritarian, even in democracies such as the USA and Britain, when compared to today. Business organizations tended to reflect other forms of already existing organization.

FAMILY　家族式

The family is probably the oldest form of social organization, and it is therefore perfectly logical that for many centuries businesses were organized along the same lines as families. Until the late nineteenth century the vast majority of businesses, no matter how large, were owned by the members of a family (the East India Company, founded in the seventeenth century, and the Bank of England, founded in the eighteenth century, are two rare exceptions). Family members not only owned the business but also served as its senior managers. The companies that resulted had strong hierarchies and placed much emphasis on control. The atmosphere was very paternalistic; the owner/managers expected unquestioning obedience from their staff, but at the same time had a responsibility to look after the people who worked for them, often in their private lives as well as at work. Family organizations have fewer divisions and semi-independent business units, and control is very much in the hands of a few people at the top.

The family model of organization remains strong in some parts of the world. Many of the powerful Chinese-owned corporations of Singapore, Hong Kong and elsewhere in South-East Asia, such as Cheung Kong, owned by the Li family, and Kerry Everbright, owned by the Kwok family, are structured along family lines, and it even still sometimes happens that alliances between companies are accompanied by marriages between members of the owning families. In southern Europe, too, family-style organizations still exist, with a single patriarchal figure controlling the company. The late Gianni Agnelli of Fiat is perhaps the most important example of such a manager in our own time.

Family organizations tend to be quite strong and yet also flexible, provided that the dominant team at the top are capable managers. When they are not, because control is so highly centralized, people lower down the organization are unable to take corrective action and fix problems because they have not the authority to do so. The current woes of the Korean company, Hyundai, whose chairman committed suicide late in 2003, are an example of this.

BUREAUCRACY　官僚式

Bureaucratic forms of organization first appeared in civic bodies such as governments and the church, and also in the army. Bureaucracies have very strong hierarchies; indeed, it can sometimes seem that preserving and maintaining the hierarchy is the primary object of bureaucracies. These organizations set much store on position and rank within the hierarchy, and senior members tend to exercise a high degree of control over their juniors. Large bureaucracies also tend to have many layers of management between the top and the bottom.

官僚式组织强调等级。

The aim of bureaucracy is to allow senior management to control the organization effectively, using a system whereby everyone knows their place and role and works efficiently to carry out that role, with individual efforts meshing together like cogs in a machine. In fact, the opposite effect is often produced: orders given at the top of the organization never reach the lower levels, or reach them in a distorted form, thanks to the filtering effect of the many layers in between. David Packard, co-founder of Hewlett-Packard, once compared managing a bureaucracy to pushing on one end of a forty-foot rope and getting the other end to do what you want.

Bureaucracies, especially large ones, are in fact very difficult to control. This has two consequences. First, it means that people within the organization can, if they choose, create power centres of their own. A particularly popular or charismatic manager will gather around himself or herself a circle of like-minded people. These in turn will use their roles and influence to gather more loyal subordinates, until in time this group is able to influence policy and strategy throughout the organization. These groups can hinder or even block policies which have been determined by senior management. When there are several of these power centres, each with its own agenda and group of loyal followers, the entire organization can become paralyzed while the rival groups fight for control.

The second consequence is that bureaucracies are particularly resistant to change. By their nature bureaucracies are inflexible and meant for stability rather than change. But the lack of control means that when change is necessary, people who wish to resist change find it easy to do so.

Bureaucracy has become something of a dirty word in management circles over the last two decades, particularly since Tom Peters and Robert Waterman's spectacular attack on bureaucracy in their book *In Search of Excellence*. Peters and Waterman (and Peters in subsequent books like *Thriving on Chaos*) called for bureaucracies to be torn down completely and replaced with new forms of organization where hierarchy and control no longer existed. While some found this to be an attractive prospect, others pointed out that a limited degree of hierarchy and control were inevitable; without these things, the result would not so much be democracy as anarchy. The British management guru Charles Handy was among those who cautioned against embracing organizational change for its own sake, and called for organizations to be configured to meet their purpose and the needs of their customers and staff.

LINE AND STAFF 直线参谋型

The line and staff organization is a modified form of bureaucracy. It too was adapted from the army, especially from the command system developed by the Prussian field-marshal Helmuth von Moltke in the 1860s and 1870s, and was popular in management circles thanks to the efforts of two early gurus, the American Harrington Emerson and the Briton Lyndall Urwick. The line and staff model attempted to preserve the best features of bureaucracy—control, reporting and information flows, clear definition of roles and responsibilities—while introducing more flexibility and cooperation between parts of the organization.

The line and staff organization has two parts: the line, or 'frontline' departments, particularly those involved in production and marketing, and the staff, advisers and experts who work with the line departments to improve methods, efficiency, productivity and so on. In the original conception, functions such as finance, research and development, human resources and the like would work closely with production and marketing to find new and better ways of working and managing. Emerson compared these two sides of the organization to the hands and the brain, the one guiding and controlling, the other actually doing.

Unfortunately, in practice the line and staff organization proved to be as inflexible as the original bureaucracies. In particular, the 'staff' functions tended to regard themselves as superior to the 'line', and instead of working co-operatively tended to issue orders and expect them to be followed. Although it enjoyed considerable popularity as late as the 1950s, the line and staff organization has now all but disappeared.

M-FORM　事业部制组织机构

M-form (the M stands for 'multi-divisional') organizations are similar to line and staff organizations, but attempt to get around the problem of the conflict between line and staff by offering the line more autonomy. The term M-form was first used by the Harvard business historian Alfred Chandler, and he credits the invention of this form to Pierre du Pont, who used it to great effect first in the du Pont chemical business and later at General Motors in the early twentieth century; but other earlier M-form businesses can be seen, notably the Medici Bank in fifteenth-century Florence (though the latter was based on interlocking partnerships and was arguably more flexible).

M-form organizations break up the business into several different divisions. At General Motors there were six divisions; Du Pont Chemicals began with three, and the Medici Bank employed four. Du Pont and the Medici divided the organization by function: at the former, each independent chemical or gunpowder works was set up as separate division, while the Medici divisions were based on financial services, wholesale distribution, woollen cloth manufacturing and silk cloth manufacturing. The divisions at General Motors were each devoted to a specific type of car, ranging from the luxury Cadillac to the cheap but reliable Chevrolet. Each division was left to conduct its business largely as it chose, so long as it met targets set by the head office. The head office itself consisted of a relatively small group of managers who set overall strategy and analyzed performance, but did not intervene in day-to-day management unless a crisis ensued.

The M-form system was only really feasible with large organizations, but it became very popular. Other successful twentieth-century companies that used it included Sears Roebuck and Standard Oil (New Jersey). It in turn evolved into the conglomerate form which characterized business from the 1930s to the 1970s, the most spectacular example of which was the Americanfirm ITT, led by Harold Geneen. M-forms and conglomerates worked, but only so long as their top management, especially the management team at head office, was of the very highest quality. General Motors was a huge success partly because du Pont was able to gather around him one of the finest management teams in world history, including near-legendary figures like Alfred P. Sloan, James Mooney, John Raskob and Donaldson Brown. But, as Jim Collins points out in his recent book *Good to Great*, great management teams never last; their members retire or move on. Something more enduring is required for lasting success. M-forms and conglomerates could not meet that challenge, and proved impossible to manage by less capable people.

DECENTRALIZED ORGANIZATIONS
分权式组织

Although M-forms represent an attempt at decentralization, the real push to decentralize came in the late twentieth century. This change can be seen as a response to two phenomena: the increasing social emphasis on the individual and the perception that democracy and free markets offered the best chance for the individual to flourish, and more directly, the growing lack of competitiveness of many American and European businesses in the face of aggressive competition from the Far East, namely Japan.

Japanese businesses were on the surface highly centralized, with strong hierarchies and strict controls. However, they also managed to have strong elements of internal co-ordination and harmony; there appeared to be little of the coercion that characterized Western bureaucracies. (At least, this was the perception at the time: when the Japanese economy ran into its own problems in the 1990s, it was revealed that Japanese businesses could be very coercive indeed.) The Western, especially American, response was to try to reshape organizations into more flexible forms, with less emphasis on hierarchy and control and more emphasis on coordination and individual responsibility.

FLAT ORGANIZATIONS 扁平组织

The first step was to 'flatten' organizational hierarchies by stripping out layers of management, usually mid-level managers, from the hierarchy. The aim was to bring the top and the bottom of the organization closer together, eliminating alternative power centres and focusing the whole organization more closely on its goals. While not actually decentralization as such, this practice did result in more individual responsibility being handed down to lower levels of the organization. Flat organizations were also more efficient in that having fewer managers on staff meant lower costs. Wholesale sackings of middle managers characterized many businesses in the 1980s and 1990s.

Not everyone agrees that flat organizations are a good thing. The Japanese management scholar Nonaka Ikujiro believes that a critical mass of management is necessary for effectiveness; too few managers and the company becomes overstretched and cannot properly conduct functions such as knowledge management (see Chapter 8). Andrew Grove, leader of the semiconductor maker Intel, also believes that a sizeable pool of managers is needed in order to ensure creativity and flexibility. The problem is that shape of the hierarchy and the number of managers are two separate problems. A flatter hierarchy has been shown by studies to pay dividends in terms of flexibility and co-ordination. The answer may be to reconfigure the organization in such a way as to allow these benefits, without necessarily shrinking the pool of management talent.

ORGANIC ORGANIZATIONS
有机型组织

One way of doing so is to conceive of organizations in organic terms rather than the mechanistic approach used in bureaucracy. Organic organizations are said to function naturally, working together in an almost instinctive co-ordination rather than requiring overt direction. Just as human beings do many basic things like walking, talking and eating without conscious effort, so organizations ought to be able to simply work together without control. Organic organizations are also in tune with their environment, recognizing its influences and adapting and evolving in response to environmental change; they thus are pre-disposed to be flexible, adaptable and accepting of change.

Organic organizations have been talked about for a long time, and comparisons of organizations and living organisms can be found in writings on governance as far back as the Middle Ages. In the 1980s and 1990s the discussion took on a new turn as increasing emphasis began to be placed on the human element in organization, especially in people as repositories and transmitters of organizational knowledge. The Dutch writer Arie de Geus, formerly a senior manager with Royal Dutch/Shell, argued in his book *The Living Company* that ideally organizations should be made up of self-regulating systems which function in natural harmony.

The problem with organic organizations is that although we can agree on their nature and how they should function, we are less certain of how to construct one, and still less of how to adapt old-style centralized organizations to the new form. Research in this area is continuing.

MATRIX ORGANIZATIONS   矩阵组织

Matrix organizations do not do away with vertical hierarchy, but instead introduce another, overlapping layer of organization based on different principles from the original hierarchy. For example, a company that has a standard functional division-production department, marketing department, HR department and so on, each reporting through a vertical hierarchy to departmental senior managers—may also institute a series of operating units based on particular products, or on specific markets. These new units do not substitute for the old hierarchy, but instead work in parallel with it. There have been some famous matrix organizations in the past, notably at computer maker DEC and at the Swedish-Swiss engineering firm Asea Brown Boveri (ABB).

The matrix organization at ABB was the brainchild of the company's inspirational chief executive Percy Barnevik, and was generally regarded as a success. ABB actually used a combination of product-based and market-based operating divisions. For example, there were turbine and electrical equipment divisions, and the managers of these operated on a global basis. But there were also specific national divisions for the USA, Britain, Germany and so on, representing all product lines in their particular markets. This structure formed the core of Barnevik's 'think global, act local' approach to business which sought to gain the advantages of globalization along with the flexibility of local markets.

Matrix organizations have their problems, though, not least of which is the fact that individual members of staff may end up taking instructions from two different managers, and when these have different priorities, conflict ensues. An early form of matrix organization employed by Edwin Land at Polaroid eventually collapsed when the 'product line units' began trying to assert primacy over the functional departments. Ken Olsen, a former Polaroid director, attempted to use the same system when chief executive at DEC, and the ensuing chaos eventually resulted in him being forced out of his job. Matrix organizations work, but only when they have strong and visionary leaders who can pull the organization together behind them.

NETWORKS 网状型

The idea of designing organizations as networks has also

been around for a long time, but has received increasing support in recent years from advances in both communications technology and neuropsychology, both of which have advanced understanding of how networks are designed and how they function. In their recent work *The Individualized Corporation*, Sumantra Ghoshal and Christopher Bartlett state that networks offer a third alternative to the problem of whether parts of the organization should be closely tied to each other or left autonomous. Rather than dependence or independence, they say, the answer is ‘interdependence’, with people, departments and business units existing separately and in a state of equality, each concentrating on their own specialism but linked by a network that ties all the parts closely together and gives them a common purpose.

Ghoshal and Bartlett list a number of organizations which have used networks successfully including ABB (above), 3M and McKinsey. There is little doubt that networks are very powerful, but again, they require strong and effective leadership; without this, there is the danger that co-ordination will fail and the organization will lose its focus.

VIRTUAL ORGANIZATIONS 虚拟组织

One of the newest forms of organization to come under scrutiny is the virtual organization, first proposed in the 1980s. Virtual organizations are much like networks but they are also geographically dispersed and are deliberately ‘fuzzy’ in nature. Not only does the virtual organization have few offices or physical facilities—its only tangible assets are people and the computers and other technology they need to process work and maintain communications—but it can sometimes be difficult to tell where the organization begins and ends. Other parties, suppliers, even customers, can be temporarily or permanently included in the organization if they are made part of its networks. Anyone can be part of a virtual organization, no matter where they are; location is no longer important.

The virtual organization has several advantages. First, it is cost-effective, with few requirements for expensive premises. Second, it is very flexible: virtual organizations can be designed, set up, changed or dismantled much more quickly than more conventional organizations. Finally, it is very responsive and can quickly adapt to changing needs or market conditions. That said, the virtual organization is not always suitable for every kind of business. It works best in areas like consulting or financial services, where the product or service being delivered is intangible. It would be impossible to mine uranium or build ships on a virtual basis; but the principles of communication and integration that lie at the heart of the virtual organization may have utility elsewhere as well. Again, experiments and research into this novel form of organization are continuing.

In the previous two chapters we have shown the relationship between business strategy and goals, on the one hand, and the structure and nature of business organizations, on the other. But this chapter has also made clear that organizations are composed of people, and it is how those people behave and interact that in large measure determines how well the organization will function. In the next chapter, we move on to look specifically at the issues involved when people work in organizations.

摘要

● 组织由使用技术工作的不同的人组成。

● 任何组织的基本结构是其内部各个不同的人之间的关系，或者通过正式的层级或者通过非正式的网络相联系。

● 不存在两个相同的组织：所有组织都受环境和它们内部的人的影响，从而产生了独有的特征。

● 组织不是静止的，它们是动态的。它们随时间改变、成长和演化，往往还会偏离其领导者的指导和控制。

● 存在许多不同类型的组织，但是合适的组织形式由其是否适合达成目标的来决定。

SUGGESTIONS FOR FURTHER READING
延伸阅读

There is a huge literature on organizations and organization behaviour, much of it highly technical. The following are (mostly) accessible:

Argyris, C. , *Management and Organizational Development*, New York: McGraw-Hill, 1971.

Even senior academics sometimes complain that Argyris's books are dense and hard to read, but this one in particular repays the time and effort. Particularly important is the section on defensive routines.

Collins, J. , *Good to Great*, New York: Random House, 2001.

A study of what makes great companies, with much useful material on how companies are organized and structured for best effectiveness.

Ghoshal, S. and Bartlett, C. A. , *The Individualized Corporation*, New York: HarperCollins, 1997.

Has some very interesting things to say about the relationship between the organization and the individuals within it.

Jay, A. , *Management and Machiavelli*, London: Hodder & Stoughton, 1967.

Fun and thought-provoking, based on the author's own experiences as a manager.

Mintzberg, H. , *Power in and Around Organizations*, Englewood Cliffs, NJ: Prentice-Hall, 1983.

A look at the dynamics of organization from one of management academia's most original thinkers.

Morgan, G. , *Images of Organization*, Newbury Park, CA: Sage, 1986.

A very powerful and readable book which shows just how complex organizations are, and how no one theory ever suffices to fully explain them.

Peters, T. J. and Waterman, R. H. , *In Search of Excellence: Lessons from America's Best-Run Companies*, New York: Harper & Row, 1982.

People either loved this book or hated it; read it and make up your own mind!

Pugh, D. S. and Hickson, D. J. , *Writers on Organization*, Newbury Park, CA: Sage, 4th edn, 1989.

A collection of short excerpts from some of the key writers on organization over the past several decades, providing a good introduction to several different views on organization.

4

HUMAN RESOURCES
人力资源

The problems of internal equilibrium are chiefly concerned with the maintenance of a kind of social organization
in which individuals and groups, through working together,
can satisfy their own desires.

（Fritz Roethlisberger）

所谓内部均衡问题，主要与某种社会组织的存在形
式有关，个人和集体通过协同工作来实现自我愿望。
——弗里茨·罗特利斯伯格

It is a truism in modern management that 'an organization's
most valuable resource is its people'. We saw in the last chapter that organizations are composed of people working with
technology, organized into various units and sub-units such as
groups, teams, departments and business units. But people
are more than just providers of labour. They are also the primary custodians of organizational knowledge, and provide the
vital spark of creativity that makes businesses innovative and
competitive. Without people, organizations would exist only on
paper.

'Human resources' is the modern term for the human
component of organization. It replaces older terms such as 'labour' and 'personnel', terms which reflected a view that people were primarily just providers of labour, either physical labour on the assembly line or 'mental labour' in areas such as

design and sales. It also reflected the old strong division between management and workers. Human resources, which began coming into widespread use in the 1970s, is a more holistic term that includes both management and labour. The management of human resources is now seen to take in a wide range of tasks, from industrial relations to training and development; in effect, anything which affects how people work within the organization.

DEFINITIONS 定义

Human resource management   Human resource management (HRM) is a specific managerial discipline which seeks to make human resources more efficient and more effective. It does so by: (1) forecasting future human resource needs and planning accordingly, (2) recruiting the best possible people into the organization, (3) appraising the performance of existing employees and managers, (4) ensuring that employees and managers are adequately rewarded and compensated for their work, (5) ensuring that the working environment is safe and conducive to effective work, and (6) ensuring that relationships within the workplace are harmonious. Human resource management can thus be seen as the interface between the business and its people.

人力资源管理

Staffing   Staffing refers to the number of staff—employees and managers—the business needs in order to be both efficient and effective. In most cases a business will seek an optimum number of staff: too few and human resources are overstretched, with a risk that work will not be done properly or at all; too many and costs begin to rise. This is a particularly tricky task if the business is growing, for it then becomes necessary to determine both the optimum level of staff now and try to predict the optimum level in the future. *Note*: in this chapter we use the term 'staff' to include both workers and managers.

人员配置

The difference between these two groups is discussed in more detail below.

Appraisal   This involves looking at individual staff members, and sometimes also at groups and teams, to see how well they are performing their duties and how effective they are being, in order to ensure that work is carried out as planned, and also in order to identify people who might be promoted or moved into other roles where they can be even more effective.

Compensation   Compensation or remuneration are terms for the rewards employees and managers receive in exchange for their work. A typical compensation 'package' includes pay (monetary earnings) and benefits, which can include free or subsidised health care, pensions, use of company-owned cars, options to purchase shares in the company, or any other benefit mutually agreed between the company and its staff.

Employee involvement   Formerly known as industrial democracy, employee involvement refers to the principle that organizations will be more effective if employees are allowed to participate in management, or at least are allowed to have greater say in management decisions and are consulted regularly to determine their wishes and views.

Industrial relations   This is a subset of human resource management activities which aims to ensure that relationships within the workplace—particularly between employees and management—remain smooth and harmonious. The prevention of industrial disputes such as strikes, and the swift resolution of these when they do occur, is the principal goal.

THE HUMAN RESOURCE MANAGEMENT DEPARTMENT 人力资源管理部门

Human resource management has become a highly specialized activity within management, and most companies of any size now have a dedicated human resources (HR) department—sometimes several of them. This has led to the view in some quarters that HRM is a separate discipline from management. However, it would be a mistake to think that HRM is not a management function at all. Managers manage people, and human relationships are at the heart of their everyday tasks.

As noted, human resource management is a function of management that aims to ensure that the human resources of the business are used effectively. But this does not mean that human resource management is there simply to make sure that employees work harder and make the company more profitable. Randall Schuler, who teaches HRM at New York University, comments that human resource management also has a strong obligation to individual employees and managers, to represent their interests when they are in conflict with those of the company and to ensure that they are happy and satisfied in their work. There is also a broader responsibility to society as a whole, remembering always that staff have wider duties and responsibilities within society, outside the orbit of their employer.

Indeed, human resource management owes its origins to a sense of managerial social responsibility and genuine need to improve the lot of the ordinary worker. The period 1890 – 1910 saw the nadir of working conditions in European and American factories, at a time when many workers also lived in immense poverty in their homes. The practice of 'sweating' labour, extracting the maximum possible labour from workers for the minimum possible reward was considered orthodox management practice. Despite legislation in the early nineteenth century, children were still often employed. Arthur Chamberlain, a consultant called into the Kynoch gunpowder works in 1890, found children of thirteen or fourteen beginning work at six in the morning; unfed at home, they were heating their breakfast over candles next to assembly lines where cartridges were filled with black powder. Fatal explosions were not uncommon. Chamberlain concluded that not only was this immoral, but it was a symptom of bad management. Companies that took care of their employees tended also to be efficient and profitable.

Not coincidentally, the same period of history was characterized by violent and bloody industrial disputes, and enlightened employers saw that time lost during strikes was eating into productivity. Better industrial relations meant more efficient working. Companies began setting up labour relations departments with the primary function of promoting industrial peace. But gradually it became clear that there was more involved than just ensuring that disputes were resolved. The realization that employees, if well paid and well looked after, would work harder and become more productive, dawned slowly over the next twenty years. In 1910, Henry Ford's car production plant at Highland Park, Michigan offered daily wages five times those of his competitors, and received thousands of applications for jobs. Ford and his managers could take their pick of the best possible employees, and the plant became world famous for its efficiency and productivity. Similarly John Patterson, founder of National Cash Register, realized that by providing subsidized meals for his employees he could improve their health and they would be better able to work and take less time off due to illness.

By 1920 labour relations had changed its name to personnel management, and was being widely taught in business schools. Research began on how employees behaved and performed in the workplace, and personnel management received its first theoretical grounding. By the 1950s, personnel management had taken on most of the functions it has today, looking after training and development, recruitment, pay and working conditions, appraisal and planning. The change to human resource management in the 1970s saw these same functions encompass management as well as employees, reflecting the growing closure of the gap between white collar and blue collar workers.

The HR department of today has a wide remit. Because organizations are composed of people, the department has a role to play throughout the organization. This importance is reflected in the fact that the senior human resource professional, usually holding a title such as human resource director, is nearly always an executive member of the board of directors; thus the HR department can comment on and influence decisions in all parts of the company.

At the same time, there are limits on the HR department's actions. First, of course, HR departments only exert authority and influence on events, people and systems inside the organization. This means that human resource managers need to watch carefully for trends and issues in society at large. Changing attitudes to work and changing behaviour more generally can cause unexpected problems. For example, it has now become acceptable for women in some workplaces to wear jeans and/or T-shirts—albeit well-made ones with designer labels—while men may well be required to wear suits and ties. This has led to a number of complaints and even lawsuits in America and Britain from male employees claiming they are being discriminated against; in many cases, the complaints have been upheld. This is a comparatively minor issue, but it can upset the equilibrium of a workplace and cause dissension between staff members that can have more serious results in future.

Second, the HR department often finds itself being required to represent conflicting interests. The wishes and needs of senior managers may not always be the same as those of junior managers or employees. This is particularly true in times of crisis, when management may need to make major unplanned changes to the organization. The good of the organization can sometimes require that the interests of individuals be sacrificed: for example, if it is suddenly necessary to close departments or lay off employees to save money so that the rest of the organization can continue to function. Individual employees who fail to live up to the needs of the business—failing to carry out their tasks properly (or at all), wasting money or scarce resources, etc.—may also have to be dismissed in order to ensure the organization itself remains effective. The employees thus affected may then call upon the HR department to represent their interests or even to get the decision reversed. This puts the department in a difficult position. If human resource managers argue the workers' case, they risk going against their own colleagues in the organization and could upset important plans. If they argue management's case to the workers, they risk being seen as the 'tools' of senior management and may incur personal resentment and distrust as a result. Being a human resource manager requires fine judgement, an ability to see both sides of a problem, and an ability to negotiate and conciliate, bringing people together to find the best possible mutual solution.

HUMAN RESOURCE FUNCTIONS 人力资源管理的职能

Human resource management consists of a number of separate tasks and functions. Many of the following will be carried out primarily by the HR department, but in consultation with other departments. Even when not directly involved in these tasks, managers need to be aware of them.

PLANNING 人力资源规划

Human resources planning tries to estimate future needs for employment. Is the company growing or contracting? If the former, it will need more employees, if the latter then fewer will be required. Assuming growth is forecast, the HR department needs to know how quickly the company plans to grow and in what areas. What special skills will be needed? What types of people will be required? What part of growth needs can be met by training and developing people already in the organization, and how many new people will need to be recruited? These are all questions that human resource planning seeks to answer.

As with most forms of business planning, human resources planning requires careful analysis and fine judgement. It is easy to say, 'Our company will grow by 30 per cent next year, so we need 30 per cent more employees.' But this may not necessarily be true. The growth might be achieved through greater productivity by the existing labour force, for example by introducing new technology. In order to forecast as accurately as possible, the HR department needs to consult with all departments and work closely with other managers to estimate human resource requirements.

Problems also arise if the growth forecasts prove to be inaccurate. If the company grows slower than forecast, the company may end up with too many employees and an excessive wage bill. If the company grows quicker than forecast, it might have too few employees to carry out all the work required, and efficiency will suffer. There are different schools of thought as to how to deal with this problem. Some managers prefer to have slightly too many employees, so that when growth comes they can quickly and easily cope with the extra effort required. Others prefer to have slightly too few employees, accepting that existing employees will be 'stretched' but feeling it is better to keep costs down.

Again, like most forms of planning, HR planning needs to be regularly checked and updated, and actual progress against the plan must be constantly monitored. Because recruitment can be a lengthy process, especially for senior positions, it is necessary to plan often for several years in advance; but at the same time, change can come very quickly, and plans must be flexible and allow for rapid response to new challenges.

RECRUITMENT 招聘

Hiring employees and managers is a major HR function. Even when the company is not growing rapidly, there is a constant need for hiring new employees, as existing employees retire, are promoted out of their existing positions, or move on to other companies or organizations to further their own careers. In a company of any size, the HR department will be continuously engaged in hiring new staff.

Recruitment consists of four basic steps. First, the job to be filled needs to be advertised. A job specification or job description (explaining the nature of the job, its responsibilities, the necessary skills, and pay and benefits) must be made public, typically through advertising in newspapers or the trade press; some businesses have a policy of advertising all new jobs internally as well. Sometimes, indeed, if it is felt that the job can be filled by people within the company, no external advertising is needed, but care has to be taken here: in some jurisdictions there is a legal requirement for all jobs to be advertised in public.

The advertisement will invite qualified persons to send in applications for the job, usually using an application form, a curriculum vitae (CV) or resumé, or a combination of the two. Once applications begin to arrive, they need to be filtered, and obviously unsuitable candidates discarded. The aim is to get down to a shortlist of a few candidates, typically between three and ten (though larger shortlists can exist if desired).

The candidates on the shortlist are then subjected to a closer scrutiny. This usually means a face-to-face interview with the applicant answering questions from a panel of human resource professionals and the management team to whom the new employee will report. Other measures for determining suitability might include role-playing exercises, intelligence tests, psychometric tests or even giving the prospective employees pieces of work to do and seeing how well they perform them.

At the end of the selection process, the selection panel determines the most suitable applicant. The fourth stage consists of drawing up a contract, to be signed by both employee and employer. This specifies the job description in more detail along with remuneration and benefits, and lays out the legal parameters of the job-including conditions under which either party would be in breach of contract or the employee liable for dismissal.

Great care needs to be taken during this process to avoid discriminating, or even appearing to discriminate, against potential employees. Nearly every Western country has laws forbidding employers to discriminate against potential employees by refusing to offer them jobs on the basis of sex, race or religion. Most have similar laws against age discrimination, and there may be other forms of discrimination which are banned as well. Managers must always check the laws of their own locale, and not assume that similar rules apply across the board—even within the same country.

Recruitment can be a complex and expensive process, and hiring a senior manager can cost tens of thousands of dollars in advertising and time spent on the part of the selection panel. Recruitment of very senior managers and specialist professionals is often contracted out to recruitment agencies, sometimes also known as executive search agencies or, less elegantly, headhunters. For a fee, often based on a percentage of the prospective employee's first year's salary, the head-hunter will conduct the entire process through to the point of issuing the contract.

PAY AND BENEFITS 薪酬和福利

The human resources function also determines the rate of pay each employee and manager will receive and any additional benefits they may receive. At higher levels, pay and benefits are often a matter of negotiation, and senior managers will ask to be paid what they think they are worth. At lower levels, pay is often set at fixed rates for certain types of jobs; in most cases this fixing of pay levels is done in consultation with employee representatives such as shop stewards. Through much of the twentieth century, many sectors, especially heavy, employment-intensive industries like mining and manufacturing, used a system of collective bargaining, with employer and union representatives meeting to fix pay rates across the entire industry. Of late this system has begun to decline, and individual companies and unions now have more leeway in setting rates appropriate to a particular workplace.

Most workers, and indeed most managers today, are paid by unit of labour: that is, by the hour, the day, the month or the year. Casual and manual labourers are often paid by the hour; office workers tend to have an annual salary divided into twelve equal increments and paid once per month. Less common is pay by unit of production, also known as piecework, where employees are paid on completion of a particular job of work. In the nineteenth century and earlier this was common in industry, but is now used only for a few kinds of freelance work.

Employees and managers can also be paid bonuses based on the performance of the firm, either for meeting individual productivity targets or, more commonly, if the company as a whole meets a certain performance target, employees will receive a share of the profits (in addition to their standard pay). Profit-sharing schemes were widespread in the late nineteenth and early twentieth century. They remain popular in parts of Europe, but did not catch on in the USA and were largely discontinued there in the 1920s and 1930s. American workers and managers argued that profit-sharing was unfair as workers who did not work hard tended to get the same reward as those who did, and preferred individual bonus schemes. European workers tend to worry less about this and generally consider profit-sharing schemes to be fair. This is sometimes seen as evidence of American individualism versus European collectivist ways of thinking.

A form of profit-sharing generally restricted to management but sometimes extended to workers as well is the employee share-ownership scheme. These come under different names in different parts of the world, but share the essential feature of offering the employees the chance to acquire shares in the company that employs them, either free as a bonus, or at discounted rates. Employee share-ownership schemes have been criticized on several accounts. In recent years some senior managers have become very wealthy through acquisition of shares in this manner, and it is felt that this might bias the judgement of managers (i. e. they will seek to boost the share price and their own net wealth, regardless of whether their actions are right for the business). Some companies with large blocs of shares in the hands of their employees have also expressed concern that, if an industrial dispute were to emerge, the employees could sell their shares to a hostile rival.

As well as monetary compensation for their labour, employees at all levels typically receive other benefits. Paid annual holidays and pensions are the most common of these, and in many jurisdictions companies are required by law to provide these benefits. Others might include free or subsidized medical care, contributions to help with moving house should relocation be necessary, subsidized meals in a company restaurant or canteen, discounts when purchasing the company's products or services, company cars or vouchers for public transport and so on. The variety of these 'fringe benefits' is almost endless, and can include almost anything that the company and its employees agree is of value and should be provided.

APPRAISAL AND PROMOTION 绩效评价和提升

Once an employee or manager has been hired, the human resources function needs to monitor that employee's progress. This is known as appraisal. Employees are formally appraised, usually on an annual basis, by the HR department and by their own managers. Self-appraisal, where employees are invited to comment on their own performance, is also becoming common. Appraisal is usually provided in the form of written comments—questionnaires are often sent to managers to fill out for each member of staff reporting to them—and these together with the employee's self-appraisal are then discussed face-to-face by the employee and managers. From this discussion emerges a final written report, and best practice encourages both managers and employees to read and sign these, signifying that they agree to the contents of the report.

Appraisal has many uses. At the most general level, it shows whether staff understand their role and function, and how well they are performing. This has an impact on how efficient and effective the organization as a whole is, for if individual staff do not perform as expected, the organization will suffer. Appraisal can also identify which staff are particularly competent and might be suitable for promotion. Finally, it gives an idea of current and future training and development needs (see below).

Great care must be taken that appraisal is not seen as a policing function, aimed solely at weeding out incompetents. Many staff become nervous during appraisals, feeling—sometimes rightly—that they are being judged. But a poor appraisal does not mean that the member of staff necessarily must be dismissed. They may need training or development to help them better understand their work, or they may need technological assistance to enable them to work better. They may simply be in the wrong job: N. R. Narayana Murthy, founder and chief executive of the Indian software company Infosys believes that the majority of staff who perform poorly do so because they are in the wrong function, and the problem can often be solved by moving them sideways into a position for which they are better suited. Even when it is clear that the employee is not suited to work for this particular employer, the resulting dismissal needs to be handled carefully and with visible equity and fairness.

Promotion needs to be handled equally carefully. One common complaint amongst those who study organizations is that companies tend to promote employees on the basis of how well they are doing their current job, not how suited they are for the one they are being promoted into. Promotion is often a reward for past good work; but a good junior manager does not always make a good senior manager. The Canadian psychologist Laurence Peter termed this the condition whereby 'everyone is promoted to his or her own level of incompetence' (also known as the Peter Principle). That is, at some point in their career people are promoted into positions for which they are not suited. The result is loss of efficiency for the company, and frustration and unhappiness for the member of staff. Promotion needs to be made with the well-being of both the person and the company in mind. Many companies link promotions to training and development programmes, ensuring that staff have the necessary skills to fill their new jobs before they begin work in them.

TRAINING AND DEVELOPMENT 培训和发展

Training and development is the process whereby the company provides its staff with the key skills they need to carry out their jobs. Given that the business environment is constantly changing, this is a very important function. Staff need to keep up with changes in the market, new regulations, advances in technology, etc. , if they are to remain competitive.

Most people come into an organization with some form of education and training already behind them, not only secondary school but increasingly university or technical qualifications as well. HR managers see these as being only the first step in a process that will last throughout the employee or manager's career. 'Career-long learning' or 'life-long learning' are terms for this continuous process.

People also have different personal requirements for training and development. Companies often see themselves as having a duty to help employees in their quest for personal growth, to the extent where some will not only provide professional training but will encourage and subsidize staff to take general education courses through evening classes, correspondence courses and so on. Some British companies offer employees free access to courses run by the Open University, a large distance-learning institution which has students all over the world.

Training and development can be provided either in-house or by external providers. In-house training was formerly very common, and remains so in some companies. Examples include the famous McDonald's University training programme for employees, or General Electric's Management Development Institute at Crotonville, New York, which every manager attends at some point in his or her career. GE spends some \$500 million each year on education and training at this centre. Other companies prefer to contract out training and development; human resources professionals and other managers will determine training and development needs, and will then contract training agencies, business schools, universities, consultants and other providers to actually run programmes. Such training and development can range from half-day seminars on specific subjects to graduate education programmes (often known as executive education) taken on a part-time basis and lasting a year or more.

DISCIPLINE 纪律

The human resources function also includes discipline, if staff violate their contracts in some way. If staff do breach their contracts, the first step is to investigate and understand the reasons for the breach. Measures taken may then range from warnings to penalties such as demotion or withdrawal of certain privileges to outright dismissal. Cases where discipline is required can include breaking the law or industry codes of conduct (such as financial market dealers engaging in insider trading), verbal or sexual harassment of fellow staff members, other inappropriate workplace behaviour such as alcohol or drug abuse, endangering the health or lives of fellow workers by violating health and safety rules, persistent absenteeism, and so on. Two specific cases which require careful handling are known as 'deviant behaviour' and 'whistleblowing'.

DEVIANT BEHAVIOUR 越轨行为

Deviant behaviour can have several meanings but is generally used to mean cases whereby employees deliberately seek to harm the company they work for, through sabotage, vandalism, theft, leaking sensitive information to rival companies or the media, or any other action that would be detrimental to the company's interests. Often deviant behaviour is conducted in secret and may be very hard to detect. Such cases are rare, but they do occur in every large organization from time to time. Managers need to be vigilant in order to spot such problems, but must avoid draconian monitoring and enforcement actions which might alienate those staff members who are innocent.

WHISTLEBLOWING 告密

Whistleblowing is a special form of behaviour that occurs when a member of staff believes that a colleague or the company as a whole is behaving illegally or unethically. There have been a number of examples of this in recent years, particularly during the series of scandals that rocked corporate America in 2001 – 2002.

Whistleblowers may indeed harm the company they work for, but they believe that they are doing the right thing. They may indeed believe that the company itself is causing such harm that it is worth paying any price to stop its behaviour. Alternatively, they may believe that if the current management is exposed and removed, the company itself can be saved.

Some whistleblowers doubtless act out of pique; they may be disgruntled ex-employees or people who bear a grudge. Others act out of sense of morality, outraged at what they see as wrongdoing around them, like the famous 'Deep Throat' whistleblower who leaked the Watergate scandal to reporters from the *Washington Post*.

How should management handle whistleblowers? Ideally, of course, the company should never get into a position where whistleblowing is necessary. If problems are occurring, then top management can give whistleblowers the chance to express their concerns in private. If, as in the case of the energy company Enron, top management itself is corrupt, then going public may be the only option. In this case human resources managers may even find themselves in a dilemma, and maybe even in the invidious position of having to take the side of the whistleblower against top management, if the former has a legitimate point to make.

WORK ENVIRONMENT 工作环境

The human resources function also has a responsibility to

maintain a healthy and safe work environment. This involves first, complying with health and safety regulations and generally ensuring that workers are not endangered or put at risk—or, at least, that risks are reduced to acceptable levels. Second, it means checking the work environment to ensure that it allows staff to be as efficient and effective as possible. The science of designing environments in this way is known as ergonomics, and can range from issues such as the design of office chairs and the height of computer workstations to the reconfiguring of power tools and machinery to reduce vibration and noise and make physical work easier.

RETENTION 留用

Preventing staff from leaving, particularly if they are highly skilled and difficult to replace, is also an important human resource function. In other words, it is important not only to get the best people, but also to keep them. Every member of staff represents a substantial investment on the part of the company, in terms of recruitment costs, training, development and so on. Experienced members of staff are also important repositories of organizational knowledge (see Chapter 8). Formal appraisal and informal contact can help managers to realize whether subordinates and colleagues are happy in their work or are thinking of leaving. If a member of staff is known to be dissatisfied, efforts can be made to solve problems and induce them to stay.

EXITS 离开

Inevitably, people will leave the company. Some reach a certain age or become chronically ill and retire. Others leave to go to better jobs elsewhere. It is important that exits be managed smoothly, as dissatisfied staff can harm the company's reputation once they leave. Some companies use exit interviews, face-to-face informal conversations with departing employees to learn more about why the latter are leaving and what problems if any may have caused their departure. Identifying and fixing such problems can help in future staff retention.

WHO MANAGES HUMAN RESOUR-CES? 谁来管理人力资源

The bulk of the formal activities connected with HRM, as described above, are carried out by dedicated HR departments. HRM is thus a 'support' function which handles the technical aspects of recruitment, pay, appraisals and so on. However, this does not mean that managers in other departments have no HRM functions. If a new team member is being recruited, it is common for the team leader to examine applications and be part of the interviewing panel, even if the applications were originally collected by the HR department. Managers' views of their subordinates play a major role in appraisal and in assessing training and development needs. Managers also play a daily, informal part in human resource management simply by looking after their needs, helping them to solve problems and finding resources they need, whether through the formally structured HR department or elsewhere. Thus to at least some extent, every manager is involved in HRM. The remainder of this chapter looks at some of the basic issues that all managers must be aware of.

MANAGERS AND EMPLOYEES 管理者和员工

We have spoken above at length about 'managers' and 'employees' as if they were two separate groups. This an inevitable consequence of hierarchy, as discussed in the previous chapter. Once businesses reach a certain size, fifty employees or more, and especially once employee numbers reach the thousands or tens of thousands, some degree of hierarchy becomes almost inevitable. Even in the most democratic of organizations, the legal requirement for a board of directors answerable to shareholders creates a distinction between the directors and others. The need for co-ordination and reporting means that even in organizations without traditional blue-collar employees, some managers will have supervisory roles over others. Whenever this happens, the potential for conflict between different levels of the hierarchy exists.

Conflicts between levels of the hierarchy are usually the result of issues directly related to work. Tasks set at higher levels of the organization may be seen as unreasonable or impractical by those who actually have to carry them out. Changes in the organization may be resisted thanks to poor communication, meaning people are unsure of why the changes are being implemented. Many other problems can and do occur. Many of these can be resolved through negotiation. However, there are two specific areas of conflict which can lead to more complex issues. These are conflicts over ethical behaviour, and conflicts over legal responsibilities.

ETHICAL BEHAVIOUR 道德行为

The ethical relationship between managers and employees has two dimensions. First, there is the responsibility that management, especially senior management, has to employees; second, there is the responsibility that employees have to management and the company that employs them. For a business to function successfully, there must be a great deal of trust between all parties, especially in modern, decentralized organizations where employees and junior managers work with less direct supervision. Those at the top need to take it on trust that their juniors will not abuse their positions for personal gain, while those at the bottom must be able to believe that the company will deal fairly, not only with them, but with customers, suppliers and society at large.

Problems begin when that trust is abused, and here the human resource issues become complicated. It is easy to say that human resource managers must always take the ethical position and take action against those who behave unethically; but ethical issues are not always so clear cut. If an employee learns that the company he or she works for has been evading payment of taxes and threatens to give the story to a newspaper, whose side does the HR department take? That of the individual employee against the rest of the company, helping to expose a story that could damage the company itself and its shareholders (who would lose money if a scandal caused the share price to go down, even though they themselves were innocent of any wrongdoing)? Or that of the company against the employee, forcing the latter to keep quiet and suppress the truth? The same dilemma will be posed for the employee's own departmental managers and immediate superiors.

When dealing with ethical issues, managers, especially human resource managers, have to avoid being caught in the middle, but they also have to avoid being seen to take sides. The final solution to the problem must be seen to be fair and equitable to all, or at least to as many people as possible. If this is not done, then trust will begin to erode.

LEGAL RESPONSIBILITIES 法律责任

Every manager and every employee has a contract with the organization that employs them, even if this is not always a written contract; employment law in most jurisdictions now recognizes verbal contracts of employment. These contracts specify pay

and benefits and conditions under which the employee may resign or be dismissed, but may have many other conditions as
well. Additionally, managers and employees alike are bound by
government-enacted laws and sometimes by specific regulations
enacted by industry bodies, such as codes of conduct for financial services companies.

When the law is definitively broken or a contract is agreed
by both parties to be breached, then the situation is usually
simple, as penalties will be spelled out. But in many cases the
fact of a breach of law or contract will be disputed by one or
both parties. Again, there is a danger that managers, especially
HR managers will be seen to take sides. This is becoming an
increasing problem as society becomes more litigious, and some
HR departments estimate that they now spend as much as 50 per
cent of their time dealing with legal issues. If the department
persistently takes the side of the company against individual employees in legal disputes, this may well arouse resentment that
will in time hamper the department's other work. But taking the
side of individuals against the company is often impractical.
Again there is a pressing need to be seen to be fair, equitable
and impartial.

THE CHANGING NATURE OF WORK
不断变化的工作性质

Another complicating human resource issue is the changing
nature of work in many sectors. Employment patterns have
changed greatly over the past twenty years. Security of employment is now gone in many industries; the old ideal of lifetime
employment with the same company no longer exists. Instead
employees and managers alike now increasingly have what are
known as 'portfolio careers', moving from job to job and company to company where their skills are most in demand and they

can be best rewarded.

Businesses, in turn, tend to hire an increasingly small core of permanent staff, and then when additional human resources are required either hire more staff on temporary contracts, or contract work out to other agencies or companies. The British management guru Charles Handy calls these new types of business 'shamrock organizations', composed of three parts: permanent core employees, temporary staff, and employees of another organization hired in under contract. For example, a computer software company might have a core of designers who are on permanent contract, bring in engineers and specialists on short-term contracts for specific projects, and contract out all non-essential work such as cleaning, catering, security, payroll management so on. Some human resource functions, especially training and development, are increasingly being outhoused in this fashion.

This lack of security and permanent employment has two consequences. First, staff turnover rates are much higher. In the 1970s, orthodox management thinking held that the number of staff who leave and have to be replaced in the course of a year should be no more than 10 per cent of the total number of staff (i. e. a company with a thousand employees should have no more than 100 leave and be replaced by new staff). This figure should include staff who were retiring and taking pensions as well as those who left for other jobs. Today the average figure is around 20 per cent, the great majority of whom leave to go to other jobs. This has financial implications, as there are significant costs involved in recruiting new staff including advertising, time spent on interviews and so on. At higher levels, the recruitment of senior staff is usually contracted out to specialist corporate recruiters or 'head-hunters', and these too have significant costs: typically, they charge the client company a percentage of the newly hired manager's first year's salary.

Second, some people are comfortable with these new portfolio careers and are able to adjust and adapt to new circumstances. Others are not, but this does not necessarily reflect their skills and abilities in other areas of their work. Without at least a degree of protection, these employees can become stressed, lose motivation and become less effective at their work. From there it is usually only a matter of time until they resign or are dismissed, becoming in effect casualties of the changing nature of work.

Not all the changes in work are negative ones, however. Two emerging working practices have the potential to make work more effective and to improve the quality of life of workers and managers.

WORKING IN TEAMS 在团队中工作

The past two decades have seen a switch in emphasis in HR practice from the individual working with technology to the individual as a member of a team, still working with technology but also working in partnership with other people. Recruiting, for example, looks not only at individual skills and abilities but also at how well the potential recruit might fit into an already existing team.

Teams, as discussed in the previous chapter, are seen as important because they create synergies and bring a variety of different skills and viewpoints to bear on a problem. But teams can also be mutually reinforcing in other ways. They offer people outlets for their own views and ideas, and even if these are not ultimately accepted, they still give employees and managers a chance to participate and discuss issues, rather than simply receiving orders and carrying them out. They can also play a role in building personal confidence and enhancing personal learning, developing skills and improving individual effectiveness. Team working has proved to be very popular and has been adapted to a number of different situations. Even automobile production, which was formerly very much carried out using continuous assembly lines, is slowly being converted to team production.

WORKING REMOTELY 远程工作

通信技术的进步正在使人们在主要经营场所之外进行某些类型的工作变得越来越可能。

Advances in communication technology are making it increasingly possible for people to carry out certain types of work outside the main business office. Laptop computers, modems and satellite communications mean that increasingly work can be carried out wherever the worker is, be it an airport terminal, a hotel room, a private house or apartment, or even in the open air. This is especially true in knowledge-intensive industries such as publishing, consulting and financial services. Many companies now recognize this and offer facilities for workers and managers who wish to spend part or all of their time away from the main office. 'Telecottaging' or 'telecommuting', as this is known, refers to working either from small satellite offices or from offices in the staff member's home.

Many value remote working as it gives them a chance to work in their own way and to their own patterns. It also reduces or eliminates time spent in commuting to and from work, making for a better quality of life. However, not everyone is comfortable with working in this way; some employees find they need the social environment of the office in order to work effectively. After the destruction of the twin towers of the World Trade Center in September 2001, a number of other nearby buildings had to be evacuated, including the New York headquarters of Merrill Lynch. Although Merrill Lynch found temporary offices elsewhere in the city, there was not space to accommodate all staff, and some staff had to work from home. Within a few days, some of these staff were reporting feeling out of touch and isolated, and were pleading for a chance to come back and work in the office. In fairness, it should be said that working remotely was forced on these staff by circumstances and was not a matter of anyone's free choice.

MOTIVATION 动机

Why do people go to work? Sociological and psychological studies of the workplace have often looked at this issue. From the perspective of these latter studies, people surrender a portion of their freedom by joining an organization and taking orders from others, in exchange for pay and other benefits that make their own lives easier. This trade-off theory of work motivation has a long history and is still widely current. According to this theory, in order to keep workers happy it is necessary to provide pay and benefits that will compensate them for the time and labour they give up.

Alternative theories suggest that people work for other things besides just wages and benefits, important though these may be. As suggested above, work offers people a chance to participate in society, and belonging to an organization helps give them a sense of their own place and identity. And, in most societies and by most people, work is also regarded as personally fulfilling. The German sociologist Max Weber, in his book *The Protestant Ethic and the Spirit of Capitalism*, argued that Western society conditions us to work, and that those who do not work are not only looked down on by the rest of us, but are also psychologically impaired in some way. All of us seek creative outlets, and most of us typically do so in the workplace. The tragedy of modern society, Weber went on, is that the work we usually find rarely allows our creative energies the chance of full expression. A later sociologist, the American Lewis Mumford, went on to condemn business organizations as 'machine bureaucracies' which turned people into servants of technology, and he saw that work was becoming a 'megatechnic wasteland' where people laboured solely for wages, the creative spirit crushed out of them.

Doubtless this is true for some people all of the time, and for more people some of the time, but it is not true of everyone. Studies of workplace motivation have shown that, often contrary to expectations, most people do work primarily for wages, ranking pay as the number one factor in taking and keeping a job. The point here is that this is true of *most* people, but not all. In fact, each of us have slightly different motivations that get us out of bed and into our offices each morning, and those motivations can change over time.

The American psychologist Abraham Maslow coined the term 'hierarchy of needs' to show how needs can change over time. The basic idea is that all human beings are motivated to undertake certain actions—including going out to work—by personal needs, ranging from the need for basic things such as food, water, shelter and so on, to more complex needs for human affection, personal self-esteem and self-realization or fulfilment. Human needs, says Maslow, form a sort of hierarchy, with lower level needs being more 'prepotent'; that is, they override other needs further up the hierarchy. These lower level needs are also, in most ordinary life, the needs most easily met. Those at or near the top are the most complex and difficult to satisfy; indeed, many people never get as far as the top of the hierarchy. He groups needs into five basic categories, from lowest to highest as follows:

1. *Physiological*: needs for food and water;

2. *Safety*: needs for shelter, housing, warm clothes, health and protection from danger;

3. *Belongingness and love*: needs for belonging to a society or group, including the need for friendship and love from others;

4. *Esteem*: needs for personal respect from other people, and also self-respect;

5. *Self-actualization*: the need to 'be all that you can

be', to fulfil one's own destiny or make one's mark on the environment and society.

Once the dominant lower-order needs are satisfied, other needs then come into play, thus creating the 'hierarchy' of needs. Where we are on the hierarchy at a given moment determines much of our motivation and subsequent actions. Let us take, for example, an ordinary workplace. Why do employees come to work every morning? In the first instance, of course, they need to earn money to buy food and pay rent or a mortgage. But once they are earning enough money to satisfy these lower order needs, what then? Some people will be content with this and will not advance further. Others, though, will find that other needs are emerging and becoming dominant. These could include the need to belong to a team or group or company (belongingness) or the pride and satisfaction that come from doing a good job (selfesteem). The company and managers that can recognize which employees are feeling these needs and then move to satisfy them by offering more stimulating and responsible work, for example, will find that these employees in turn become more loyal, more efficient and more productive. The potential stars are those driven by self-actualization; if they can be identified and given scope to grow, they can turn into great and transforming leaders. Such persons are, however, rare.

EMPLOYEE INVOLVEMENT 员工参与

One of the discoveries to come out of research in this field over the past century has been that people feel more motivated to work hard if they also feel that they have some say in the decisions that affect them. One of the pioneers in this field was the Quaker chocolate-making firm of Cadbury Brothers (now Cadbury-Schweppes), which rose from humble origins as a small manufacturer in Birmingham, England to become a global leader in the chocolate market in the space of about thirty years.

Cadbury Brothers used several methods of ensuring involvement, including company suggestion schemes where employees could put forward ideas for improvement, and works committees with representatives from both management and the shop floor, which debated and discussed new initiatives. Cadburys found that employee involvement, or industrial democracy as it was then known, had two benefits. First, it demonstrated to employees that management was committed to listening to them and taking their views into account when making decisions. Second, and as a consequence, employees were prepared to make serious suggestions for improvements to products and processes, and a considerable amount of innovation was generated in this way.

Other companies over the years have developed methods of employee involvement in their own way. Sometimes some unusual gimmicks have been employed. In the 1920s the Czech shoe manufacturer Tomas Bat' a gave all staff, including himself, pagers so that anyone could contact anyone else (a crude forerunner of today's in-company e-mail systems). Bat'a also felt that rather than staff having to come to him, he should go and see them, so he installed his office in an elevator, moving up and down between floors in the factory as required. In Chapter 2 we mentioned the radical experiment at Semco in Brazil, where Ricardo Semler has delegated virtually all authority to his staff and simply trusts them to get on with it. Other companies have adopted less radical means, usually but not always enabled by new communications systems like e-mail and mobile phones. Intel has won plaudits for its culture which not only enables but encourages employees to make their views known, on any subject of importance to the company, and has created a climate where people can speak their minds freely without fear of punishment or retribution.

Some theorists explicitly link employee involvement with democracy in the political sense, arguing that just as democracy has been proven to be the best way of governing society in general, so too it should be the ideal way of managing a business. Others argue that not all institutions can be run democratically (the army is a frequently cited example), and some degree of authoritarian control is necessary and desirable in business. The most common view, and indeed practice, is that consulting employees is not just desirable but essential, especially when major changes are being planned; many studies show that employees are much less resistant to change when they have been consulted about it in advance. At the same time, full democracy is difficult to implement. Shareholders demand, and regulations increasingly require, that some named person or people in the organization are responsible for its actions and accountable for its failures. Those people in turn require a degree of compliance from others around them; otherwise, they would be held accountable for actions for which they were not responsible, and very few people are prepared to accept being put in this position. Democracy in business organizations is desirable, but it also has its limits.

INDUSTRIAL RELATIONS 劳资关系

The balancing of the needs and demands of employees and those of the company comes to the fore in industrial relations. This field first deals with maintaining good relations between the company and the people who work for it, particularly those at lower levels in the hierarchy, and second, when disputes arise, ensuring that these are solved as quickly as possible and with little cost to those involved. So important is this field that many companies have specialist industrial relations managers who do nothing else but look at these issues, and industrial relations is sometimes taught in business schools as a subject separate to mainstream HRM.

Industrial relations is often seen as a confrontational area, with the company's managers looking after the company's best interests while the workers' representatives—typically, shop stewards and other officials from trade unions or labour unions—fighting the corner of the employees. Each seeks to gain advantage over the other, rather like lawyers in a courtroom. When no agreement can be reached, the dispute escalates into full-scale industrial action, typically a strike where workers withdraw their labour and refuse to work until their demands are met.

This is the popular perception of industrial relations, but it masks a much wider field of activity. In actual fact, few industrial disputes reach the level of intensity described above. Much of the industrial relations manager's time is taken up with trying to head disputes off and resolve them before they become major issues, and with trying to identify potential areas of dispute before they happen. Three key activities in this area are *negotiation*, *conciliation* and *arbitration*. In negotiations, the industrial relations managers and the workers' representatives sit down around a table and discuss problems or potential problems and reach a mutually acceptable solution. In conciliation, where a dispute is already taking place, the industrial relations managers seek to understand whatever grievance has led to the present dispute and try to resolve it to mutual advantage, often with the assistance of a third party mediator. In arbitration, both parties agree to submit their dispute to a mutually acceptable third party who will weigh up the facts and reach a judgement, by which both parties will abide. Most Western countries have independent arbitration services, sometimes sponsored by government, which will provide conciliation and arbitration facilities.

The aim of industrial relations, then, is not to fight the company's corner against its employees, but to ensure harmonious relations between management and workers. It thus fits into the larger picture of human resource management, the purpose of which is to ensure that the company's human resources are employed efficiently and effectively. This in turn requires that employees are motivated to work and committed to doing their best for the company that employs them, and that some, at least, are inspired by more than just the need to take home a pay cheque. Good human resource management is synonymous with a well-managed and efficient company.

摘要

● 人力资源是组织和其员工之间的结合点。

● 尽管人力资源管理的许多正式职能是由人力资源部门行使的，但人力管理涉及每个管理人员。

● 管理人员对为其工作的员工有强烈的道德和法律责任。

● 工作和工作场所的性质不断改变，并且管理人员今天面对的管理比过去更灵活和流畅。

● 理解使人工作的动机对于理解员工行为和态度是关键的。

SUGGESTIONS FOR FURTHER READING
延伸阅读

Adler, N. J. and Izraeli, N. D., *Competitive Frontiers: Women Managers in a Global Economy*, Cambridge: Blackwell, 1994.

Good studies of women in the workplace are still strangely lacking; this is one of the best and most readable.

Cadbury, E., *Experiments in Industrial Organization*, London: Longmans, Green & Co, 1912.

It may seem strange to recommend a book that is more than ninety years old to today's students, but this is probably the most original book on human resource management ever written. Some of its ideas are of course a product of their time and seem dated, but others are so innovative that one can only wonder why they are not still practised.

Handy, C., *The Age of Unreason*, London: Business

Books, 1989.

Handy is usually thought of as a writer on organizations, but this book is particularly good on the dilemmas facing people inside organizations.

Katz, H. C. and Thomas, A. K. , *An Introduction to Collective Bargaining and Industrial Relations*, 2nd edn, Boston: McGraw-Hill, 2000.

A good introduction to industrial relations, with a useful bibliography.

Maslow, A. , *Motivation and Personality*, New York: Harper & Bros, 1954.

A book of psychology rather than management, this work has been very influential. The chapters on the hierarchy of needs are particularly worth reading.

McGregor, D. , *The Human Side of the Enterprise*, New York: McGraw-Hill, 1960.

An important and influential book which showed the necessity of taking human behaviour into account when examining how businesses are run; influenced by Maslow (above).

Peters, L. J. , *The Peter Principle*, London: Pan, 1969.

An alternative look at human resource management, showing some common and classic mistakes.

Schuler, R. S. , *Managing Human Resources*, St Paul, MN: West, 1995.

A good basic human resource textbook with plenty of information on practices and techniques.

5

MARKETING

营　销

There is only one valid definition of a business purpose: to create a customer.

(Peter Drucker)

企业的目的，只有一个正确而有效的定义：创造
客户。

——彼得·德鲁克

If human resource management is the interface between the
business and its people, then marketing is the interface with another equally important group, customers. Put simply, marketing is how businesses attract and keep customers, who in turn
pay for goods and services, which renders the business profitable and enables it to exist and grow.

One important thing to note about marketing is that it is
proactive. Companies cannot wait for customers to come to
them; they must do something to attract customers and to make
the latter aware of the goods and services that are on sale. This
does not necessarily mean high-profile brands and advertising,
although of course these frequently do occur. But other, much
more subtle means can be used to attract and hold customers.

It is now generally accepted that businesses cannot do without marketing. Definitions of what marketing is and how it is
carried out have changed over the past century, but the basic
notion that marketing is about getting and keeping customers in

order to ensure profitability remains a constant theme.

DEFINITIONS 定义

客户

Customers At the simplest level, a customer is anyone who purchases goods or services from a business. Customers who have already made one purchase and then habitually come back to purchase more goods and services from the same business are known as 'repeat customers', and are often considered more important than those who simply make one purchase and never return. People who are not currently customers but who have the potential to become so—that is, could be persuaded to buy—are termed 'potential customers'. Customers must in some cases be distinguished from consumers (see below).

消费者

Consumers Consumers are those who actually use (consume) a product or service. In some cases, such as retailing, customer and consumer are usually one and the same person (though even then there are exceptions, such as people buying goods and then giving them as gifts). In other cases, however, the customer and the consumer are quite different. This is particularly the case when businesses sell to other businesses, which in turn sell goods on to consumers. For example, publishers rarely sell books directly to readers; they sell through intermediaries such distributors, wholesalers and booksellers. The latter are the customers, the readers are the actual consumers. The publisher must take both these groups into account when marketing: the distributors and book stores who actually pay for the books, and the consumers who read them. Even though the latter do not pay directly, their end custom is essential for the whole process. Consumers who are not customers are sometimes also known as 'end-users'.

消费行为

Consumer behaviour This is an umbrella term which includes a whole range of personal motivations, thought processes, decision-making and action on the part of consumers. Predicting and understanding consumer behaviour is one of the greatest challenges facing marketers.

Goods   Goods are what a company produces for sale. 商品
Finished goods such as cars, soap powder, clothing, computers, books and so on are known as 'consumer goods', as they are intended to be delivered to an end-user. Components and raw materials—semiconductor chips, rolled steel, automotive driveshafts, processed chemicals and so on—are known as 'industrial goods' as they can only be sold to other businesses, who will use them to manufacture consumer goods; on their own, these products are of no value to the consumer. Goods are usually divided into products and services.

Products and services   Products, in marketing terms, 产品和服务
are physical and tangible items such as computers or soap powder. Services are intangible, such as banking and financial services, insurance and so on. Many services are actually a mix of product and service: for example, a restaurant meal consists of intangibles such as atmosphere, the way customers interact with the restaurant staff and so on, and tangibles, the food and drink which are consumed; and many products also contain a service element, such as the after-sales service and warranty. In such cases, if a classification is necessary, it is usually done by the dominant element provided to the customer. Thus a car is a good, but car repair is a service: soap powder is a good, but laundry and dry-cleaning are services, and so on.

The distinction between products and services is a useful one to make when determining how a good will be marketed, but it is important not to treat this as a hard and fast rule. It is also important to consider the bundle-of-benefits concept, below.

Bundle of benefits   Regardless of whether the good pro- 利益捆绑
vided is a product or a service, the customer expects certain benefits when making a purchase. These benefits are also known as the value received by the customer. The bundle-of-

benefits concept recognizes that customers are often motivated by more than one need when making a purchase. A customer who buys a hamburger may do so for no more complicated a reason than that he or she is hungry, but a customer who goes out for an expensive restaurant meal will want more than just good food; he or she will expect good service and a pleasant atmosphere as well. Cars, which have been extensively studied, are well-known examples of complex bundles of benefits: customers may be looking for any or all of style, comfort, safety, mechanical reliability and fuel economy. Knowing that a product can offer more than one benefit to customers is critical when designing new products.

销售

Selling　　Selling is sometimes confused with marketing. In fact, the term 'selling' refers to the transaction itself, the act of selling goods to customers and ensuring that customers pay for them in return. This is not always as simple as it sounds, and the act of generating a single sale can range from simple, instant transactions (buying a bar of chocolate in a corner store) to long and complex transactions that can take months to complete (selling an Airbus passenger jet to an airline). Marketing includes selling as one of its primary activities, but has many other fields of activity as well, as will become clear below.

THE PURPOSE AND AIMS OF MAR-KETING　营销的宗旨和目标

Marketing aims to connect businesses with their customers, to the mutual advantage of both. Although more than fifty definitions of marketing have been put forward, the idea of 'meeting customer needs profitably' has stood the test of time and remains the most common definition of marketing. This remains true whether we talk of marketing as a business process, an outlook or mindset on the part of the company and its managers, or a philosophy of social exchange. There has been debate over which of these three things marketing actually is, but the consensus which has built up around the work of leading marketing academics such as Philip Kotler is that it partakes of all three.

At the most practical level, marketing is a process or function. The primary aim is of course to generate sales in order to bring money into the business. But in order to do this successfully, marketing has also to do several other things. It must first try to determine what it is that customers want and need, so that appropriate products and services can be designed and delivered. It must monitor changing customer wants and needs to make sure that products and services evolve to keep pace with changes. It must look for new potential markets that the business could enter. And, of course, it needs to monitor current customers to ensure that they are getting the value that they expect so that they will continue to make purchases. At higher levels the marketing function can become more complex, encompassing long-range market forecasting and global marketing planning; but always, marketing remains essentially focused on customers, who they are, what they want, and how the business can meet their needs.

In the 1960s and 1970s, academics like Peter Drucker, Theodore Levitt and Philip Kotler argued that businesses needed to adopt a 'marketing orientation'. Formerly, businesses had thought of themselves primarily in terms of what business they were in; that is, a company that operated railways conceived of itself as a railway company. Levitt referred to this as 'marketing myopia', and he and the others argued that a company needed to define itself in terms of who its customers are; in this view, a company that operates railways should see itself as a transportation company, as it is transport that customers need, not railways *per se*. In the 1990s Gary Hamel and C. K. Prahalad took this a step further by arguing that companies should define themselves in terms of their core competencies, that is, the things that the company does well and that are highly valued by customers. To have a marketing orientation, or market orientation, means nothing more than that the company should always focus on its customers and their needs, as customers are the ultimate source of value.

MARKETING AND SALES
营销和销售

Marketing was originally thought of as synonymous with sales. Indeed, when the first marketing departments were established, they were usually subordinate to the sales department (today, the position is often the other way around). But in the first decade of the twentieth century, two American academics challenged this notion. The first, Walter Dill Scott of Northwestern University, applied the principles of psychology to marketing, especially advertising, and realized that rather than selling directly to customers, advertising could be scientifically designed to stimulate people to make purchases; in other words, rather than the business going out to its customers and persuading them to buy, the customers would come to the business of their own volition. It was Scott who wrote the first texts on what we now call consumer behaviour. The second was Paul Cherington of Harvard Business School, who looked at the variety of factors that influence customers when buying goods, and realized that a range of issues, including price, availability and product quality, came into play. Marketing, then, was more than just a matter of selling goods; it was also about designing goods that would sell, delivering them to the right place to make it easy for the consumer to buy, and stimulating demand through promotion.

Sales remains an important marketing function, and Peter Drucker's view that 'marketing makes selling superfluous' by stimulating demand so that goods sell themselves is a hard one to realize. At some point the transaction has to be made, and in most industries this still requires personal contact with the customer (although technology is changing this; see the section on e-commerce below). Philip Kotler's description of selling as 'the tip of the marketing iceberg' is perhaps more accurate. In order for selling to work effectively, a whole host of other marketing activities must precede it.

MARKETING SERVICES　营销服务

In the definitions section above we noted that a difference is usually made in marketing between products and services. For many years it was doubted whether marketing could be applied to services at all, and it was not until the 1960s and 1970s that academics such as Christopher Lovelock, Valerie Zeithaml and John Bateson began showing how the basic principles of marketing could be applied to services as well as tangible products.

When reading through the remainder of this chapter, the reader should be aware that although the marketing of services does follow those basic principles, there are two key ways in which services differ from products. First, services cannot be stored, and there are distinct limitations on the times and places at which they can be delivered. Second, the customer is always part of the service process. These two issues make the marketing of services a somewhat different issue than the marketing of products.

SERVICES CANNOT BE STORED
服务无法储存

It is not possible to keep an inventory of services in the

same way that it is with products. By and large, customers consume services when and where it suits them. In many cases the service has to be delivered where the customer is, either because of emergency (roadside assistance to motorists whose cars have broken down) or because that is what the customer wants (home delivery of shopping, pizzas, etc.). In some cases a compromise is necessary, such as restaurants, where the customer comes to the premises of the business providing the service, or health care, where people go to see their doctor or to a hospital.

The issue of time is even more critical. Consumers use services when it suits them, not when it suits the company. People want to eat when they feel hungry; they go to doctors when they feel ill; they go to garages when their cars break down; they have their hair cut when they feel the need to do so.

This leaves marketers of services with a dilemma. Services that are not used are wasted; they cannot be stored for another occasion. A restaurant may be open between ten in the morning and noon and have only 20 per cent of its tables occupied. Between noon and two p. m. , however, the occupancy rate may run at 100 per cent. The concept of efficiency would suggest a simple solution: close the restaurant between ten and twelve, when few people are using it, and remain open between twelve and two when the full capacity can be sold. The services marketer would reply that those using the restaurant between ten and twelve may be few in number but they are regulars and generate a steady income. The period between twelve and two may be very efficient in terms of service, but the restaurant may also be turning people away, thus losing potential customers. Further, those who are eating during this period may not be enjoying the experience as much as those who came in the morning; some people enjoy eating in a full, busy, noisy restaurant, but others do not.

This is a simplification of a complex phenomenon, but the

basic issue is that while marketers of products will typically strive to sell 100 per cent of the business's output, those who market services know that it is impossible to do so. They concentrate instead on ensuring that the capacity needed is available when required. A secondary activity is managing demand, smoothing out peaks and troughs of demand and trying to ensure a more even level of take-up of services by customers. In the example above, the restaurant might offer special deals on meals during the morning period, hoping to persuade a few customers to switch their custom to this period and ease the pressure on the prime period after twelve. Similarly, hotels will offer lower prices mid-week, to encourage people to stay with them at off-peak times; airlines offer special deals at low times, retail outlets hold sales in January and so on.

THE CUSTOMER IS PART OF THE SERVICE 客户是服务的一部分

Even more importantly in the eyes of many is the fact that the customer is in effect part of the service. Customers themselves play a role in nearly every service. They consume meals, they use healthcare services, they learn in classrooms, they provide the hair that hairdressers cut, they choose the goods they buy in retail outlets. Customers are not passive: they choose what they want and when they want it. In doing so, they interact with members of staff provided by the business, and it is the interaction between them that determines the success of what marketers call 'the service encounter'.

The key point is this: the service is not what the business provides, it is what the customer receives. It is the customer's use of the service that makes it a service. Services marketers have another phrase for this: 'the customer is part of the factory'. A service that is offered but is not used is effectively not a service at all; no transaction has taken place, the seller has not been met by a buyer. It requires a customer for a service to be completed.

SPECIAL FEATURES OF SERVICES MARKETING 特色服务营销

The marketing of services, then, has some special features. First, services marketers need to work very closely with what are known as the contact people, the people who actually deliver the service (waiters, mechanics, hairdressers, etc.). These contact people themselves have much responsibility for marketing, as they are in closer contact with customers than anyone else in the business. How they present themselves, how they interact with customers and what they actually do determines the quality of the service and closely affects customer satisfaction.

Contact people make the difference between good service and bad service, and marketers have a responsibility to support the contact people and ensure that they know what is expected of them. Some writers on services marketing speak of the contact people as 'actors', who work to a 'script' prepared for them by marketing. Sometimes this really is a script (like the waiter who arrives at your table and says, 'Hello, my name is Mark and I will be your waiter for this evening') but more often it is a looser set of guidelines showing contact people how they can provide the best service in any given set of circumstances. The script helps contact people know what to do in order to provide the appropriate service.

Finally, because the customer is involved in the production of the service, and the customer cannot be controlled—customers, according to the theory above, bring their own 'scripts' to the service encounter, and these sometimes conflict with those provided to contact people by the business—it is not possible to satisfy every customer all the time. Even if the service is provided exactly according to specification, some customers will have different expectations and will feel unhappy or let down. This is known as service failure. To deal with service failures, marketers design recovery procedures. When a customer is known to be unhappy (such as a hotel guest complaining of uncomfortable beds), or it can be reasonably assumed that the customer is unhappy (such as a passenger on a late arriving plane), well-managed firms have systems for dealing with this. Unhappy hotel guests can be offered apologies, a different and better furnished room, a voucher for a future stay at the hotel free of charge, or any of a number of other benefits. Passengers on a delayed flight can be offered free or discounted tickets for future journeys. By offering effective compensation for the original problem, the services marketer can convert a dissatisfied customer into a satisfied one. Paradoxically, some studies have shown that customers who experience service failures and then are well compensated through the failure recovery process sometimes end up more satisfied than their fellow customers for whom everything went right!

CUSTOMERS　客户

As the preceding sections of this chapter have hopefully made clear, customers are the focus of the marketing effort. Virtually everything in marketing is done with the customer in mind. Marketers know that, quite simply, the business depends on its customers. Without them, there is no revenue, and no profit.

In order to get and keep customers, therefore, marketers spend a great deal of time trying to understand them. They use many tools derived from psychology, neuropsychology and sociology, as well as research done within the field of marketing itself. Marketers are still learning about consumer behaviour, in particular about how consumers make decisions, and knowledge in this field is still regarded as incomplete. Doubtless marketers will never fully understand how their customers behave and think—but this does not mean they should not continue to try to expand the horizons of their knowledge.

BEHAVIOUR   行为

If marketers can correctly forecast what consumers will want, when and where they will want it, and what prices they are willing to pay, then marketers can design and deliver successful products and services. All too often they cannot, and thus it is that the launch of each new product is highly risky. Consumer behaviour is also susceptible to change: fashions in clothing or cars, for example, may change and once-popular products thus become obsolete.

There is a direct relationship between the degree to which marketers can understand and predict how consumers will behave and react, and the level of risk the company faces in marketing. The more we know about our customers, the better we will be able to match our goods with their needs. So marketers spend a great deal of time studying their customers and what they do. Among the activities marketers look at are when and where people make purchases of particular goods; the frequency with which repeat purchases are made; how much they are willing to pay; what features they value about a certain type of goods; what current fashions may be motivating particular types of purchases; the kind of lifestyles that customers lead; and so on.

As well as existing customers, of course, marketers also look at potential customers, that is, people who are not currently customers of the business but could be induced to become customers. These people might be customers of competitor firms, in which case the marketer needs to know what it is about the rival firm that people value. Or they might not be currently buying this good at all, in which case the marketer must determine why this is so and what could persuade them to change their mind. For example, a customer with a television and a VHS video recorder might be a regular buyer of videocassettes. Might this customer be persuaded to convert to DVD and begin buying these products instead? To answer the question, the marketer has to look at some of the barriers that might prevent people from switching from video to DVD (cost, concerns about quality, etc.) and whether and how these might be overcome.

CUSTOMER DECISION-MAKING
客户决策

To marketers, the human brain is a black box, its workings invisible from the outside. Until an effective technology for reading minds is developed, marketers can only understand consumer motivation and decision-making in a very general way.

At the heart of consumer behaviour is the decision-making process. Two questions are asked here: why do customers make decisions to purchase (or not purchase), and how do they make those decisions?

The 'why' question is the most difficult one to answer. Marketers study theories of human motivation, like the hierarchy of needs discussed in Chapter 4; commonly used to explore motivation in the workplace, it can also be used to understand motivation in the marketplace. According to this theory, people will be motivated by different needs at different times; when they are hungry they will buy food, but when their need for food has been satisfied they will move on to higher-order needs such as the need for love or for self-esteem, which might in turn lead to purchases of jewellery or attractive clothes.

At a more micro level, marketers also study why consumers

purchase particular items. Why pick one product over another quite similar product, or one brand over a nearly identical brand? Why buy Nike instead of Adidas, McDonalds instead of Burger King? Answers can often be found in neuropsychology and psychology, exploring how our brains react to often very subtle cues. Certain shapes, colours or words may convey messages, often subconscious, that influence our decisions. Sometimes these cues vary between cultures: in the West, for example, red is a colour associated with strong emotions, danger, even anger, while in China it is associated with love and power. One of the problems most frequently encountered when marketing internationally is that consumer behaviour varies between cultures.

Motivation, though, is by no means the only factor in answering the 'why' question. Individual perception, personality, attitude and background knowledge all play major roles. These things cannot be predicted, nor in many cases can they even be measured with any degree of accuracy.

'How' questions are somewhat easier to study. There are several models of consumer decision-making, all drawn to some extent from psychology but verified both experimentally and through practice in marketing. One of the most widely used of these is the AIDA model. AIDA stands for awareness-interest-desire-action and suggests that consumers go through a four stage process when making a decision:

- *Awareness*—the consumer becomes aware of the possible range of goods that might satisfy a particular need, scanning the environment and mentally cataloguing the different possibilities.

- *Interest*—of the available options, the consumer eliminates those that are less satisfactory, and focuses on one or a few that are likely to be most satisfactory.

- *Desire*—the consumer has now decided which option will be most satisfactory, and passes from a passive understanding or appreciation to an active desire for the good in question.

- *Action*—following on awakened desire, the consumer then takes steps to make a purchase.

Advertisers have long been aware of AIDA, and use it to design advertising copy that appeals to as many of the four stages as possible. 'Honest Ed's car showroom is now open for business. Best cars in town. The solution to all your transportation needs. Come down and see us now!' is a crude example of this, but great advertising tends to be much more subtle. One of the most famous ad campaigns of all times, 'Coke is it!', partly designed by the late president of Coca-Cola, Roberto Goizueta (coincidentally, Mr Goizueta's mother was named Aida), appealed to all four stages in just three words, accompanied by some simple images of laughing, happy young people quenching their thirst by drinking Coke. In a split second, the viewer was reminded of the existence of Coke, interest was stimulated by the images, an information cue was passed to the effect that, if the viewer was thirsty, Coke would quench the thirst, and the need for action was correspondingly awakened. 'Coke is it!' was instrumental in defeating the challenge then being mounted by Coke's rival, Pepsi.

AIDA is not the only model of decision-making. There are others, such as ACU, or attention-comprehension-understanding, which relates to how consumers acquire information about goods without actually proceeding to purchase them, or ATR, awareness—trial—repeat, which focuses on consumers who make repeat purchases. All these models have in common the notion of consumers first gathering information, then making a choice, and finally proceeding to action.

CUSTOMER SATISFACTION
客户满意度

As well as understanding why consumers make purchases,

marketers also look closely at how happy customers are once they have made a purchase. It is assumed that every customer, when making a purchase, has certain expectations of that product. The customer parted with his or her money to buy a good in order to meet a certain need, or group of needs. These needs can be more or less complex, depending on the product. When buying a soft drink, the customer is usually thinking along the lines of 'I need this to quench my thirst', although in the case of more fashionable drinks, image 'I need this to give myself credibility in the eyes of my peers' may also play a role. When buying soap powder, similarly, the customer is motivated by the desire to get his or her clothing clean. When buying a car, however, the needs become more complex, and the customer may sum up his or her needs along the lines of 'I need a safe but stylish car which will be mechanically reliable and have good fuel economy but also be comfortable to drive' (other issues like colour or the presence of a sunroof or CD player may also enter into the mix).

When the customer makes the purchase, he or she then carries out what is known to marketers as a post-purchase evaluation. Of course, few of us as customers think of it in those terms; we think of it rather as making up our mind whether we like something or not. Basically, three outcomes of this process are possible:

1. The customer does not receive the value that he or she expected; the good purchased falls short in some way of what is wanted and does not wholly satisfy needs. There is then a gap between expectation and value received. This result is known as dissatisfaction.

2. The customer does receive the value that he or she expected, and the good purchased matches needs exactly. There is no gap between expectation and value received. This is known as customer satisfaction.

3. The customer receives all the value he or she expected,

and then receives additional value over and above that expected; other needs which the customer had not considered are also fulfilled. This excess of value received over expectation is known as customer delight.

Customer delight is what marketers would achieve in an ideal world. However, this cannot be done by simply building on extra product features that add value. Some of these features might not necessarily result in customer delight; customers might instead be baffled or irritated by features they did not want or did not ask for. Adding extra features also raises costs, and customers may be reluctant to pay a correspondingly higher price. Achieving customer delight requires fine judgement and understanding of what customers truly value; and of course, this will be different not only from product to product but also from customer to customer.

CUSTOMER RETENTION 留住客户

Another area of concern for marketing is customer retention. This means ensuring that customers, having visited the business's premises or bought its goods once will continue to do so. This is important, as research has consistently shown that it is repeat customers who provide the majority of revenue in almost every industry. Further, from the perspective of the business, it is much more expensive to get customers than it is to keep them. Persuading people to buy in the first place is an expensive business, requiring substantial investment in research, advertising and other promotions. Keeping them, however, is usually a matter of ensuring continued customer satisfaction (although advertising and promotions can play a role in ensuring that customers remain loyal, particularly if competitors are trying to woo them away). The American academics W. Earl Sasser and Frederick Reichheld argued some years ago, in articles in *Harvard Business Review* among other places, that 80 per cent of revenue is provided by 20 per cent of customers. Focusing on these customers and ensuring they remain loyal is a major area of marketing activity.

MARKETING RESEARCH 市场调查

The terms 'marketing research' and 'market research' are in practice used interchangeably, but in fact have slightly different meanings. Properly speaking, market research is the study and analysis of markets, usually with the aim of determining the current state of the market and what changes may be about to occur, and then the study and analysis of consumer behaviour within the market. Market research can itself be divided into two primary types, strategic and behavioural. Questions commonly asked in economic market research include:

- the total size of the market; how many actual and potential customers there are, what volume of products are sold, how much revenue is generated;
- the rate of growth in the market; typically in terms of percentage points per year;
- who the major competitors are, and what market share each has; that is of the total of customers, sales, etc., what percentage is accounted for by each competitor;
- who customers are, what their disposable income is, and what their buying patterns might be, including frequency of purchase;
- the likelihood of new competitors entering the market;
- the likelihood of major changes in the market or in competing products thanks to new innovations, technology, etc.;
- where the best opportunities might lie for any business seeking to enter or expand in the market.

The information generated by this research is then considered when formulating marketing strategy (see below). Much of strategic marketing research is known as 'desk research' and involves trawling through previously published material in print or through the Internet, although telephone interviews with major competitors, distributors and so on are also commonly used. For this reason, businesses frequently contract out strategic market research to independent agencies, so as to keep their own identities secret.

Behavioural research looks at customer behaviour and decision-making as described above. Behavioural studies conducted by university or business school academics will often look at behaviour and decision-making in general terms, but that conducted by businesses, or by agencies on their behalf, usually focuses on the business's own primary markets. Within those markets, the business seeks to understand what product or service features are valued by customers, what stimulates them to make purchases, and how they choose between competing products and services when buying.

Behavioural research is often qualitative rather than quantitative; that is, it seeks to generate in-depth information from a relatively small number of people, rather than large-scale data that can be analyzed numerically. (The difference between data and information will be discussed in Chapter 8.) Information can be gathered through a variety of methods. Postal questionnaires are cheap and easy to mail out, although response rates are often very low; usually only a small minority of those to whom questionnaires are sent can be bothered to fill them out and send them back. Facetoface interviews, either conducted quickly on street corners or in more depth in an office or interview room, can also generate information from individuals about their own preferences. Focus groups, discussions with a small group of customers or potential customers led by a researcher, can also be helpful in that the synergy of a group discussion can throw up ideas that might not come out in individual interviews. However, great care must be taken when putting together a focus group to ensure that a variety of views are fairly represented.

Behavioural research uses small 'samples' of the population, ranging from a few dozen to a few thousand at most; research using larger groups is usually too time-consuming and too expensive. How this sample is chosen is a matter of major concern, and must reflect the key questions the business wants answered. For example, if the business wants to find out how its current customers are feeling, it can choose a random sample from its customer database (assuming it has one), which should give names, addresses and details about products purchased and so on. If it wants to study prospective customers, then the issue becomes more complicated. There are databases of the population at large, and of specific segments of the population, which can be purchased from agencies, but some companies use simple public databases such as telephone books or voter registration lists.

A further kind of behavioural research is known as post-purchase research. This seeks to analyze how satisfied consumers are once they have made their purchase. If evidence of widespread dissatisfaction is uncovered, then the marketing department needs to rethink its strategy.

A new kind of market research which is still in its infancy, despite widespread availability of data, is the analysis of actual customer buying patterns. Through EPOS (electronic point of sale) systems, it is now possible to analyze when, where and how customers make purchases in considerable detail. EPOS has generated vast amounts of data since its first introduction, but the problem is that few businesses have the time and resources to analyze this in full. Analyzing EPOS data can be particularly valuable for confirming the information customers give through interviews or questionnaires. What people say they will buy is not always the same as what they do buy, and identifying the gaps and understanding why they occur can lead to a still better understanding of consumer behaviour.

MARKETING STRATEGY
市场营销战略

Marketing strategy is a subset of strategy (see Chapter 2) which decides how marketing resources should be allocated and what objectives should be set. Some writers make a distinction between marketing strategy, which looks at marketing objectives only, and strategic marketing, which integrates marketing into overall corporate strategy. Others hold this to be a meaningless distinction.

Marketing strategy is of course as varied as business itself, but at the most basic level we can say that marketing strategy decides the following:

- what segments of the market the business will concentrate on;
- what goods will be offered to the market, and at what price;
- how goods will be distributed and reach the customer;
- what methods of promotion and advertising will be used and what resources will be devoted to this.

These decisions are then written into a marketing plan.

SEGMENTATION 市场细分

When marketers speak of segments, they are talking of specific groups within the population at large. Segmentation is carried out so as to try to identify the group of people most likely to become customers. This allows the company to target its advertising and promotional activities more effectively by appealing directly to this group rather than trying to design 'one size fits all' promotions.

Segmentation defines people by certain characteristics, such as age, geographical location, social background, income, lifestyle and so on. The most effective form of segmentation uses several of these characteristics together. A famous method of segmentation is by socio-economic class which groups people by income and lifestyle into the categories A, B, C1, C2, D and E. Class A consumers are well-to-do and are primary purchasers of luxury goods, while Class E consumers are the poorest strata in society with little purchasing power. This system has been around for a long time—Aldous Huxley satirized it in his novel *Brave New World* in the 1930s—but is still in widespread use today. Postcode or zipcode segmentation, which assumes that people sharing a common postal address will have roughly similar tastes and values, is also in widespread use.

Segmentation is also partly determined by the product or service being sold. Starting with the basic classifications mentioned above, marketers then try to determine which groups their goods are most likely to appeal to. An alternative approach is to look at the market, determine which groups have the most disposable income and are mostly likely to consume, and then design products or services that can be sold to that market. A combination of the two is also possible: the marketer might start with a basic good or range of goods, assess several market segments, determine which is likely to be most profitable, and then adapt the goods to fit the needs of that market.

Often segmentation begins as a process of elimination, knocking out groups of people who are *not* likely to become customers—women over sixty rarely buy sports cars—and then gradually narrowing down to the groups seen as most likely to buy. Segments can be as small or as large as seems reasonable. Examples might range from all women over forty, all families with children, or all car drivers, to affluent young men, teenagers living in the New York area, or people interested in extreme sports. The choice is up to the marketer, so long as the goods being offered will fill the needs of this particular segment.

MARKETING PLANS 营销计划

Marketing plans are documents which set out the marketing strategy, including what segments the company will target with what products, and what resources will be devoted to this effort. Marketing plans generally set targets for sales and revenue. Once the plan has been set in motion, actual sales or revenue growth is monitored and checked against the targets set in the plan. If sales or revenue fall short of the targets, then clearly something has gone wrong; either the plan has not been properly implemented, or the targets were set wrongly in the first place. A revised strategy or even a completely new strategy may then have to be developed.

Marketing plans, like most plans, tend to work on a planning cycle, with new plans developed at regular intervals, anywhere from six months to two years apart. Some companies prefer what is known as 'rolling planning' with plans constantly being revised and updated as time passes. It is also common for plans to exist for several different time periods: there might, for example, be a long-range plan that looks five years into the future, and within the framework of this plan, one or more short-range plans covering the next six months or year.

BOX 5.1 FOUR PS OF THE MARKETING MIX

- *Product* : what products and services are delivered to customers;
- *Place* : where and how the products and services are delivered to customers;
- *Price* : what the customer will be required to give in exchange for products and services;
- *Promotion* : how customers will be made aware of and encouraged to buy products and services.

PRODUCTS AND SERVICES
产品与服务

One of the most famous methods of determining marketing strategy involves planning for what are known as the 4Ps: product, price, place and promotion (also known as communication). Since this model was developed in the 1960s at Harvard Business School, the marketing of services has become a major issue, and thus we should correctly be speaking here of goods (products, services, or a mix of the two). But to stay faithful to the original model and preserve its alliteration, we will temporarily refer only to products. The reader should be aware that the comments in this section apply to services as well.

Products are what the business sells to its customers, and thus they are central to the process of marketing. Without them, the business has nothing to offer and can earn no revenue. It sometimes happens that new businesses start up and do not yet have finished product for sale, but they must at least have an idea for such a product, otherwise they will find it impossible to raise money to get started. In such cases, the business will be under pressure from its investors to bring a finished product to market as soon as possible.

The matching of products to customer needs is a major focus of marketing activity. Companies can either design a product and then search for a market segment to sell it into, or they can look at likely and affluent market segments and the needs of consumers in those segments and then design products to fit those needs. Often, as noted above, there is a combination of the two activities, with basic products or groups of products adapted to meet emerging new markets or changing tastes in old ones.

There are different types of products, and the distinction between goods and services is just one of many. Some of the following classifications may be encountered:

- *Industrial products*—these are products which are only sold to other businesses, never to consumers. Either they are raw materials, or they are large capital purchases such as cargo ships and wide-bodied passenger jets for which there is no public demand.
- *Luxury products*—these are top-of-the market products such as luxury cars, clothes, suitcases, jewellery, etc. The market for these is primarily the A classification of consumers, as they are the only ones with the disposable income to afford these products on a regular basis. Class A consumers know this, of course, and regularly purchase luxury products to confirm their own status in the eyes of their peers.
- *Fast-moving consumer goods (FMCG)*—these products are used on a regular basis and frequently consumed, making regular repeat purchases necessary. Laundry soap and breakfast cereals are two classic FMCGs that have been widely studied.

PRODUCT LIFE CYCLES 产品生命周期

Every product has what is known as a life cycle. When first introduced, the product is seen as new and exciting by customers, and can be marketed as a novelty. People will pay higher prices for this novelty, and the product will be highly profitable, although the costs of developing the product in the first place may still have to be paid for.

As time passes, the product reaches what is known as maturity. Competitors, seeing the success of the product, may introduce their own versions of it. The novelty buyers, willing to pay high prices, will move on to the next new thing, and in their place will come a different type of customer, more conscious of value for money and less willing to pay higher prices. However, there are generally many more of these customers than there are of the novelty buyers, so the business can safely reduce prices to meet the demands of this new group of customers.

Finally, the product reaches what is known as saturation. The majority of people who might reasonably be expected to purchase the product have now done so. Sales growth remains static or even begins to decline. Responses to this situation can include reducing the price still further to stimulate sales, adding new features to the product, withdrawing the product from its core market and trying again in another market, or withdrawing the product altogether and ceasing production. The latter, of course, requires that other products be available to fill the gap.

A very few products never reach saturation. Most of these are fast-moving consumer goods, where repeat purchase is a major factor. Some brands of laundry soap and breakfast cereal have been on the market for over fifty years; Kellogg's Corn Flakes and Coca-Cola are both more than a hundred years old.

NEW PRODUCT DEVELOPMENT
新产品开发

The tastes, wants and needs of customers are constantly changing, and this means that marketers have to spend time developing new products if they are to stay abreast of consumers. New product development is typically undertaken in collaboration with the research and development (R&D) function of the business (see Chapter 6), but marketing plays a pivotal role in understanding current and future customer needs and passing that information to the rest of the company. Although brands that last for fifty or a hundred years do occur, they are rare; the majority of brands have a lifespan of less than ten years, and for many it is less than five years. There is also evidence that product life cycles are shortening and products are becoming obsolete more quickly, as the pace of technological innovation quickens; even as the first DVD players were coming onto the market, companies in Japan, the USA and Europe were already beginning research on a successor technology (as yet unnamed) that will make the DVD obsolete. New product development must thus be a constant and continuous activity if marketing is to stay in touch with the market.

新产品开发是一个长久持续的活动。

PRICING 定价

The art of pricing a product or service for the market is a fine one. Two factors come into play. First, there is the need to make a profit; that is, the product or service must sell for more than it cost to make or provide. The finance and accounting side of the organization will often ask that this margin of profit (the difference between cost and price to the customer) be as large as possible, in order to maximize overall profitability. Second, there is the price that customers will find acceptable. If the price is too high, few or no customers will buy it, especially if there are lower priced alternatives on offer. If the price is too low, then paradoxically many customers will not buy the product or service either, believing that cheapness sends a signal of poor quality or lack of value. The concept of 'value for money', often a major factor in consumer decision-making, works both ways. Customers expect to pay a fair price and not be ripped off, but at the same time they believe that if goods are priced cheaply then they are probably also made cheaply and will not provide value. Ideally, the marketer seeks to find the level at which the greatest amount of profit will be generated per sale and, simultaneously, the greatest number of sales stimulated.

为产品和服务定价是一门艺术。

One of the major issues to consider when setting prices is sensitivity. A term borrowed from economics, sensitivity indicates how customers will react when the price of a good changes. If customers will react at once to even small price changes, meaning that sales rise sharply if the price falls and drop sharply if the price goes up, the good is said to be price-sensitive. If there is very little reaction to price changes, then the good is said to be price-insensitive. This is in part a function of how conscious of price customers are when making their purchasing decision, and also of the number and quality of alternative products on the market. Rolls-Royce cars are price-insensitive because raising the price even by several thousand dollars would probably make little difference to sales. If a bank raises its mortgage interest rates by half a percentage point above those of its competitors, however, borrowers will leave in droves, switching their mortgages to other lenders; mortgages are thus very price-sensitive.

There are many different approaches to pricing. Price skimming involves introducing new products at a high price and then gradually lowering the price in order to attract more customers. Discounting involves lowering prices in order to increase the volume of customers. Predatory pricing involves undercutting competitor prices so as to win market share away from them; there may be legal restrictions on predatory pricing in some jurisdictions.

PLACE　地点

Place refers to where the goods are sold and how they reach the consumer. For manufacturing companies, place is usually referred to as distribution, or sometimes logistics, and encompasses the delivery of finished goods from the factory gate to the customer. The great majority of manufacturing companies contract out their distribution to independent firms; others set up semi-independent subsidiaries.

For retail and service businesses, the issues are different;

'place' here has a more literal meaning. Most of these do not deliver directly to the customer, instead the customer comes to them. But customers are not always willing to travel long distances to shop, and thus these businesses have to find locations at outlets that suit their customers. This is why shops tend to cluster in certain locations, such as high streets of small towns, retail parks and so on; these are locations that customers are known to favour. Site selection is thus a very important activity for retailers in particular, who need to be in prime locations where customers will find them easily. One measure of a site's desirability is 'footfall', that is, the number of people who go in and out of the store regardless of whether they make a purchase. A store with a high footfall is obviously in a location that customers find easy to reach, and it therefore has a larger number of potential customers.

For these retailers, however, there is still the physical problem of distribution to solve. Goods do not arrive in shops of their own volition; they must be transported to the shops. A variety of solutions are possible. An arrangement can be made with the manufacturer or the latter's distributor to ship goods as needed directly to each retail site, but this is complex and uncommon. More common, at least for the moment, is a system whereby the retailer has a series of central distribution sites where goods are brought together, warehoused and then sent on to the retail outlets as needed. Companies try to keep the quantity of goods stored in this way to a minimum because these goods have been paid for but not yet sold and thus represent money sitting idle.

Of course, not all retailers and service providers have shops. Some do business through mail order, over the telephone or by Internet, and then deliver goods to customers. Again, a variety of methods of doing this are used. Pizza delivery companies use messengers in cars or on motorcycles or bicycles to deliver from the kitchen to the customer's home. Mail order clothing companies use the ordinary post or courier companies to deliver goods ordered. Florists have industry networks whereby a company in one location undertakes to fill orders placed in another location; thus a customer who phones her florist in New York can have flowers delivered to her mother in California, provided by a different florist.

A very few goods, mostly financial services and knowledge-based products can be delivered directly over the Internet, a single mouse click transferring the good from one computer to another. In the late 1990s some writers prophesied that in the end all business would be done this way. Sadly, however, no one has yet figured out a way to deliver a pizza over the Internet, and for the time being at least this method of delivery is likely to affect only a few industries.

COMMUNICATION 沟通

沟通或促销是指企业使客户了解其产品和价值的方法。

Communication or promotion is the means by which the business makes customers aware of its goods and the value they offer. Communication is probably the most complex aspect of marketing, and is also probably the hardest to get right. It both depends on other elements of marketing and influences them. Failed communications can result not only in lost sales but bad publicity for the business as a whole; successful communications can make the company hugely profitable.

Every communication of no matter what type requires four elements:

- *The communicator*—the person sending the message (in this case the business and any advertising agencies working on its behalf);
- *The message*—the information that is to be conveyed to the audience;
- *The channel*—the path by which this is conveyed to the audience;

- *The audience itself*—in this case, potential customers.

When designing communications, marketers can usually take the first and last elements as given. They will know who and what the business is, and thanks to prior efforts in market research and planning, they will know at least in outline form who and where the audience is. It is the message and the channel that are the most problematic.

Getting the message right is tricky because in most cases the marketer has only a limited amount of time and space in which to attract the customer's attention: thirty seconds of television airtime, a quarter of a page of newspaper space, a single sheet of paper pushed through a letterbox, a small segment in the evening news, etc. , depending on the type of promotion (see below). In that short space or time, they must convey as much information as possible about the good, the company providing it and the value it offers to customers; ideally it should also seek to stimulate a purchase, as in the AIDA model above.

The channel is equally important. As Marshall McLuhan famously said, ' the medium is the message '. Tests have shown that people not only have different perceptions of goods advertised on television from those advertised in newspapers, but also have different perceptions of goods advertised in different newspapers. People will view an advertisement in *Business Week* rather differently from one appearing in the *National Enquirer*. More prosaically, there is the matter of which channels or media people use. If it is known that a significant number of potential customers read *Business Week* but very few read *National Enquirer*, then the former would appear to be a natural choice of channel. If it were to be known that potential customers read both indiscriminately, then advertising in both might be sensible; the appearance of the ad in the second channel would validate the first and provide readers with more cues and stimuli to purchase.

With those basic points in mind, communications with customers or potential customers can be divided into four main types:

广告

- *Advertising*—advertising is communication through the mass media for which the company has paid. It can include radio and television advertising, newspaper advertising, billboards, websites or any other form of media. Companies design their own advertisements, or more typically employ specialist advertising agencies to design these for them. Advertising is designed to appeal to a large group of potential or actual customers, and not directly to individuals. Extremely expensive to design and place, advertisements rely on reaching the largest possible audience in order to ensure their effectiveness.

直销

- *Direct selling*—this is personal selling, either face-to-face, over the telephone (telemarketing) or by post or e-mail (direct mail). Unlike advertising, direct selling attempts to appeal to an individual; the message can be tailored to the needs and buying habits of the individual by engaging in conversation or, in the case of direct mail, subtly changing the message that goes out to different groups of consumers (for example, different messages may be sent out to consumers living in different postal code areas). Direct selling attempts to stimulate a rapid consumer buying decision, whereas advertising lays the information in front of consumers and assumes the latter will make the decision in their own time.

促销

- *Promotions*—sometimes known as 'below-the-line' promotions—media advertising and direct selling are conversely 'above-the-line' promotions—this class of communication is based on a range of incentives that can include in-store advertising, price discounts, coupons or vouchers offering discounts on later purchases, 'buy one get one free' offers, offers by the seller to make a charitable donation for each purchase and so on; there is virtually no limit bar the inventiveness of the marketer. These promotions are usually aimed to stimulate volume sales, and are particularly common with fast-moving consumer goods. They are often undertaken in conjunction with other types of communication such as advertising or direct selling.

- *Publicity*—publicity refers to the placing of news stories in the media—television, radio, newspapers, magazines and so on—which give positive information about the business and its products and services. Unlike advertising, the business does not pay directly for these. Publicity campaigns are very important in certain industries, notably publishing and films; film producers rely to a large extent on favourable publicity generated by reviews, magazine profiles of film stars and so on to create public interest and bring people to see their films.

宣传

BRANDS 品牌

A brand is a good, and more than a good. It brings together the whole bundle of benefits and ties these to an easily recognizable image or logo. Successful brands are considered very valuable for their ability to attract and retain customers.

品牌价值

It is sometimes popularly assumed that the brand *is* the image or logo: that the Nike brand is simply the 'swoosh' symbol, or that Coca-Cola is simply the famous red and white logo. In fact, these are merely the outward symbol of the brand. The reality of the brand is all the qualities and benefits that consumers associate with those symbols, including utility, style, reliability, quality and so on.

The Coca-Cola brand is based not only on the red and white logo, but on the design of the containers in which the drink comes—the famous curved Coca-Cola bottle became a style icon, and is still in use in some parts of the world—and the taste of the drink. Famously, when Coca-Cola tried publicly to change the recipe of the drink, customers objected and deserted the brand in thousands, and did not come back until the recipe was restored. Coca-Cola's managers protested that not only had the recipe already been changed many times to keep pace with changing tastes, and that the recipe also differed in other parts of the world (Coke in Asia often has more sugar than in Europe, etc.), but to no avail. People had their own image of the brand, and when the company changed that image, the brand lost its appeal.

Brands, then, are very subtle things. They cannot be created overnight; they take a long time, often years, to emerge. They are built on: (1) a combination of goods whose features have been carefully tailored to the needs of a particular market, (2) carefully designed and targeted promotions that spell out these features and link them to the brand image and logo, and (3) the willing participation of consumers who 'buy into' the brand by accepting the linkage and supporting the brand. This latter is very important; the best designed brand in the world will fail if consumers do not accept it. A brand can only be a brand if consumers see it as one.

Because brands take so long to develop and have many development costs, not least in advertising, it is important for the business to get as much value out of the brand as possible. One way to do this is to try to ensure 'brand loyalty'; that is, once consumers have a chosen a brand, they will want to stick with it as long as possible. There is an entire sub-set of marketing theory which deals with brands and ensuring brand loyalty. The manufacturers of famous brands such as Coke and Nike of course do not sell their products directly, but instead sell through a complex network of distributors and retailers. This entire network is mobilized in order to attract and keep customers. The famous 'cola wars' of the 1980s and 1990s, when Coca-Cola and Pepsi sought both to keep their own customers loyal and to win customers away from their rival, saw not only some of the most expensive advertising campaigns in world history, but also a whole range of promotional and publicity activities undertaken by retailers and others, usually in concert with the main rivals.

MARKETING ACROSS CULTURES
跨文化营销

Another problem which all marketers face is the problem of marketing from one culture to another, or marketing the same product in different cultures. There has been for some time a considerable debate about the importance of culture and whether it should influence marketing practices. Proponents of global marketing believe that globalization is leading to convergence in people's tastes, customs and manners, and point out that products like music CDs, films and running shoes can already be marketed to virtually the same segments the world over.

Others, however, believe that localization is essential, as many cultural barriers remain and brands which have instant recognition and appeal in one culture meet with incomprehension in others. The Nova car, manufactured by General Motors in the USA and its European subsidiary Vauxhall, was very successful in North America and Britain. But when the car was sold into Spanish and Latin American markets, it was an utter failure. Why? Because Nova, or 'no va' in Spanish, means 'doesn't go'.

Even brands which appear to be global are recognized differently in different countries. Kentucky Fried Chicken, which in the USA is seen as a family eating place, in Europe is largely the preserve of young people and in China is seen primarily as a favourite place for children's birthday parties. De Beers, the world-wide marketer of diamonds, has been expert at coming to terms with different perceptions of what is essentially a uniform product. In North America and Europe, diamonds equate with romance, so De Beers markets diamonds for engagement and wedding rings and as gifts to loved ones. In Japan, notions of courtship and marriage are different, so De Beers turned instead to marketing diamonds directly to affluent women, to adorn rather than to give to others. In China the perception was different again; De Beers was able to come back to the wedding ring market, but here the emphasis has been on the longevity of diamonds, as a symbol of a long and lasting marriage rather than courtship and romance.

While the academic debate about globalization and localization in marketing carries on, in practice most companies adopt a mix of the two. Global marketing has many advantages. It allows resources to be concentrated in order to achieve a bigger budget for, say, advertising; this means that more and better ads can be produced, and probably more cheaply than if every national subsidiary did its own ads. Big international businesses usually start off with a global marketing strategy, and then tailor elements of it where necessary to meet different local needs and conditions. This policy of 'thinking global, acting local' appears to be the most successful response to the problem.

BUSINESS-TO-BUSINESS MARKETING 企业对企业营销

Business-to-business (B2B) marketing (marketing to consumers is sometimes known as B2C) is often regarded as a special subset of marketing activity because of the different nature of the customer. Business customers have different motivations from ordinary consumers, and different wants and needs as well. Business customers usually have a much clearer idea of what it is they want, and will often go to suppliers with exact specifications; it is up to the supplier to then work to develop a product that will meet that specification. Business customers are also fewer in number, and it is usually possible to develop a much more detailed customer database with information about each customer's characteristics; this makes highly individualized marketing possible. Personal selling remains a major form of marketing communication in this area.

Of late, the emphasis in business-to-business marketing has been on developing long-term partnerships between customers and suppliers. This is both a means of creating repeat sales, with all the benefits of customer retention noted above, and of ensuring close contact between buyers and suppliers so that the latter can meet the former's needs more exactly. These long-term relationships form a crucial part of just-in-time supply management (see Chapter 6).

NON-PROFIT MARKETING
非营利营销

For many years, it was believed that marketing could be applied only to businesses. But Philip Kotler's work on marketing in the late 1960s showed that marketing can be used in a variety of situations where profit is not involved. Charities and governmental agencies providing health, education, Third World aid and a whole variety of other worthy causes can also use marketing to raise money and create awareness of their causes. Kotler's breakthrough in this field was to show that virtually anything could be a 'product'. If people cared about their children's education, or their own health, or famine victims in Ethiopia, the charity could meet their 'need' to do something about this by promoting better education, doing research on cures for cancer, sending food aid overseas and so on.

What the charity then had to do was market this 'product' by promoting it and themselves in very much the same way as a business would. Kotler showed how, with very little adaptation, the basic principles of marketing discussed above could be used to market good causes without a profit needing to be involved. This view was heavily contested when Kotler and his colleagues first introduced it, but is now accepted as orthodox thinking, and nearly every major charity has professional marketers on its staff. Health care institutions and universities have similarly taken marketing on board.

Marketing works for non-profit organizations because the heart of marketing is the direct connection between consumer and supplier. Profit is involved in business marketing because there is an economic imperative to make money; so the *purpose* of marketing for businesses is to make a profit. But the purpose is not the same as the thing itself. In any kind of marketing, the ultimate aim is to allow an organization to contact its customers, users or consumers. If marketing does not reach its audience, it fails. If it does reach the audience, then it can be put to any purpose the organization desires.

摘要

● 营销是企业与其客户之间的接触面，没有客户企业将没有收入和利润。

● 营销既是一种具有某些任务和责任的职能，又是思考市场和客户的一种方式。

● 了解客户的行为和客户如何做出决策是成功的营销最重要的一步。

● 一旦理解了这一点，那么企业就必须设计满足客户需要的产品，以客户愿意支付的价格送达指定的地点，同时促销那些货物的可用性使客户了解并感兴趣购买。

● 为了使营销适合不同的消费群体、不同的文化甚至一种利润动机不是最重要的情况，营销必须灵活。

SUGGESTIONS FOR FURTHER READING
延伸阅读

Alberts, R. C. , *The Good Provider: H. J. Heinz and His 57 Varieties*, London: Arthur Barker, 1973.

This biography of Heinz, one of the great marketing men of all time, not only shows marketing principles in action but is an entertaining and thoughtful study of an inspirational business leader.

Bateson, J. E. G. and Hoffman, K. D. , *Managing Services Marketing*, Fort Worth, TX: Dryden, 1998.

One of the best textbooks on services marketing, showing the differences and similarities to 'traditional' marketing of tangible products.

Kotler, P. , *Marketing Management*, Englewood Cliffs, NJ: Prentice-Hall, 1997.

The classic textbook on marketing, much of which is devoted to methods and tools. The opening two chapters define marketing and set out the basic concepts, and are worth reading as an introduction to the subject.

Levitt, T. , *The Marketing Imagination*, New York: The Free Press, 1983.

After Kotler, Levitt is probably the world's best-known marketing guru, and this book about the creative aspects of marketing contains many thoughtful ideas.

6

PRODUCTION

生　产

（1）To make an ever-increasingly large quantity of goods of the best possible quality, to make them in the best and most economical fashion, and to force them out onto the market.

（2）To strive always for higher quality and lower prices as well as lower costs.

（3）To raise wages gradually but continuously—and never to cut them.

（4）To get the goods to the consumer in the most economical manner so that the benefits of low-cost production may reach him.

（Henry Ford's fundamentals of business）

以最经济的方式将商品提供给消费者，这样他们将直接受益。

——亨利·福特的商业原则

Production is about making things, which are then sold to customers in exchange for money. The production department was once regarded as the heart of the business, the single most important element in any business organization. Today, the marketing orientation has changed this view, but production remains a vitally important element. Without an efficient and effective production department, the promises marketing makes to customers cannot be fulfilled, or at least not at a profit.

The purpose of the production department or departments is

to produce the goods customers need, in the right quantity, at the right quality, at the right time and to the right cost. Meeting all four of these objectives requires careful planning and commitment of resources. It is easy to concentrate on one of these needs to the detriment of others: for example, getting the quality right but taking too long to complete the job, or overrunning on costs. All four targets must be met if the marketing aim of meeting customer needs profitably is to be fulfilled.

There is always a certain amount of creative tension between production and the other functions, especially marketing, human resource management and finance. Production requires investment, while the finance function seeks to control costs; how much investment is put into production is often a series of constant negotiations between the two departments. Production requires skilled labour, and must make its needs known to the human resources department, which then has to find the people production needs. Most problematic of all, marketing will demand products that meet customer needs, and production must find a way of providing them without at the same time the costs becoming excessive. The relationship between marketing and production can be particularly problematic, but neither function can do without the other; one determines what is made, the other actually makes it.

More, better and cheaper are the words which every production manager hears. The pressure is there to produce a higher volume of high quality goods while simultaneously driving costs down. In difficult times, production management becomes a matter of squaring the circle. As a result, production managers are often engaged in near-constant innovation, seeking to improve both the goods they make and the processes by which they make them.

The bulk of this chapter deals with manufacturing, that is, the production of tangible products. However, a long section at the end deals with the production of services. The previous chapter discussed some of the basic issues in the production of services from a marketing perspective; here we will look at services in a little more detail.

DEFINITIONS 定义

Some of the following terms will be encountered in any study of production systems.

生产过程

Process　　Process is a generic term for how things are made. It can be applied to individual stages of production, or to the whole production system. For example, brake units for cars are manufactured through a process. Completed brake units are installed in cars through another process. The whole business of making components and assembling them into a finished automobile can also be referred to as a process.

流量

Flows　　Flows are a production concept that describes the movement of raw materials, parts and finished goods through the production system, either a single manufacturing facility or a group of facilities. Flows are often mapped using diagrams known as flowcharts, useful aids for planning and studying production systems. The complete flow, from raw materials and components into the company to finished products coming out and being delivered to customers, is known as the supply chain.

效率

Efficiency　　We defined efficiency generally in Chapter 1, but in production efficiency has two specific connotations: the elimination of waste, either of time or materials, and reliability in terms of output from production systems. Reliability in turn reflects the performance of machines—how well do they work, how frequently do they break down—and people—do they work efficiently, are they on hand when required, etc. An efficient system is one which is reliable and minimizes waste.

质量

Quality　　Quality refers in the first instance to ensuring that the product or service meets a pre-determined standard, and is consistently made to that standard without variance or defects. There are two key tasks involved: first, setting the standard accurately, and ensuring the standard is adhered to. We will discuss quality in more detail below.

Resources　Resources are what production requires to make products. They include raw materials and parts, labour and technology. People, using technology, turn the materials and parts into finished products. Thus a combination of resources is required for production. 　资源

FACTORS OF PRODUCTION
生产要素

The first theoretical considerations of how goods are produced came from the writings of economists such as Richard Cantillon and Adam Smith in the eighteenth century. These writers believed that there were three 'factors of production', inputs required to achieve an output, or in other words necessary ingredients for the making of things. These were:

- *Land*—land was seen as particularly important for industries such as agriculture and mining, but it was also necessary for setting up factories. The location of factories was particularly important when machinery was powered by water power or steam, as it had to be close to fresh water. 　土地

- *Labour*—labour was initially seen as the 'brute force' that made goods, with or without the aid of machinery. But from Adam Smith's time onward, the importance of skilled labour also became recognized. In other words, labour was not just muscle and hands, but thinking intelligence as well. 　劳动力

- *Capital*—capital originally meant simply money, required to build and maintain facilities such as farms, mines and factories. Any business venture required capital, but manufacturing ventures required large amounts of it to build machinery 　资本

and power sources.

As time passed, however, other factors began to be acknowledged. During the nineteenth century economists such as Nassau Senior, Charles Babbage, Karl Marx and Alfred Marshall all acknowledged the role that knowledge played in making production effective (see Chapter 8). By the late twentieth century the idea that 'knowledge capital' played a role in production was becoming widely accepted: as well as investing money, businesses also brought knowledge and skills to bear on production. Further, management itself began to be seen as a factor. Early theories had focused on the business owner (the 'promoter' or 'entrepreneur' in early literature) as merely a provider of capital. In the 1920s, the Austrian economist Joseph Schumpeter asserted that business owners, and by implication managers, were a more active force, serving as catalysts to get production going, and monitoring and guiding its progress. The Austrian-born American management guru Peter Drucker, influenced by Schumpeter, took this still further, asserting that management is the central focus of any business. We see, then, that production is ultimately not a matter of labour and machines, but of management.

THE INDUSTRIAL REVOLUTION
工业革命

Two great events have changed the nature of production. The first of these was the Industrial Revolution, which saw the mechanization of production. Prior to the Industrial Revolution, most production had been done on a craft basis. In craft production, businesses were small and a single individual would often be responsible for production of an object from start to finish; for example, a pair of shoes would be made by a single shoemaker. Beginning in the British textile industry in the 1770s and gradually spreading to other industries and then, in the early nineteenth century to other countries such as France, Germany and the USA, the Industrial Revolution changed the dominant mode of production to what we now call a 'line' basis. Production became concentrated on assembly lines, each of which might employ tens or even hundreds of workers, each of whom was responsible for one stage of production only. Thus in mechanized shoe-making, one worker might make patterns, one might cut out the sole, a third might cut out the uppers, a fourth might operate the machine that sews the parts together and so on.

At the heart of this new industrial process was what economists call the division of labour. Instead of a single worker taking charge of most or all of the production process, that process was broken down into a series of tasks. Each worker was responsible for a single task within the larger process. This meant in turn that work became highly specialized, especially as machinery became more complex; the range of each worker's knowledge was reduced, but that knowledge also had to be more detailed and specific. The famous system of scientific management, developed in the USA around the turn of the nineteenth and twentieth centuries, took this division of labour and specialization to extremes, breaking down tasks into the smallest possible parts and then redesigning tasks to make work more efficient.

THE ELECTRONIC AGE 电子时代

The second great event was the dawning of the electronic age, especially the advent of computers. Computers were first used to handle financial and accounting systems; the first computer to be used in a business setting, the LEO (Lyons Electronic Office) by the British company Lyons in the 1950s, also had the ability to store records of inventories of goods. During the 1960s and 1970s, advances in the technology resulted in systems such as computer-numerical control (CNC), which meant that precision machines could be guided by pre-set computer programmes rather than the human eye and hand, and this in turn reduced errors and waste. The first robots were introduced onto production lines in the late 1970s, in Japan and Sweden. Finally, advanced communications technology offered the opportunity to link machines and create entire computerized production systems.

The increasing reliance on technology meant that the nature of labour changed. Much specialized work was now being done by machines. The emphasis of human labour turned to controlling and guiding processes, rather than carrying out laborious tasks. This in turn meant that work became less repetitive and more involved in monitoring and problem-solving; also, a single individual could manage a wider range of tasks within the overall process. This has led to what the Czech-American scholar Milan Zeleny calls the 'recombination of labour'. That is, from the extreme division of labour with a focus on specialized tasks, we are moving back towards a system where people take on multiple tasks and require a broader range of knowledge. The balance between the factors of production-land, labour, capital, knowledge, management—is thus constantly shifting and changing.

MANUFACTURING STRATEGY AND PLANNING 制造战略和规划

The process of making goods for sale requires strategic thinking and planning just as any other area of business. Manufacturing strategy requires two key sets of decisions: *structural* decisions which concern what will be made and how, and *infrastructural* decisions which determine what support and resources will be required.

STRUCTURAL DECISIONS　结构决策

The primary structural decisions concern capacity. Simply put, management must decide what products will be made, when they will be made, and where. All these decisions are made with several factors in mind. The primary aim must be to make goods in such a way that they will be available to customers when the latter want them, and thus information and feedback from the marketing function of the business is very important when making these decisions. The issue of quantity of goods to be made is particularly critical. If too few goods are produced, sales will be lost and disappointed customers will go elsewhere, unless new goods can be produced very quickly. If too many are made, goods will sit in warehouses for lengthy periods of time until they can be sold. Getting this decision right is particularly difficult for complex goods that take a long time to produce, such as precision instruments or aircraft.

Once capacity decisions have been taken, managers need to determine what production facilities will be required. Again, location can be a significant issue, depending on where customers are. The cost of transporting goods from the factory to customers needs to be taken into account. In modern manufacturing, most large companies use a number of different production facilities in different locations, taking advantage of issues such as access to markets, access to skilled labour and other resources, and so on. An increasing trend in recent years is for businesses to relocate production from Europe and North America to places such as South America or China, where skilled labour is available at a much lower cost.

Another set of decisions concerns the process by which goods will be made, and in particular technology requirements. Processes need to be designed to ensure maximum efficiency and effectiveness in order to achieve the required capacity at the best cost. (The best cost is often but not always the lowest cost; sometimes a higher level of spending can achieve better results in terms of efficiency and effectiveness.) The decisions about processes are inextricably linked to those about technology, as virtually every process will depend on technology to some degree.

Once the nature and volume of the finished products have been determined, a further stage in planning calculates what components and raw resources will be required, and in what quantities. One important structural decision which must also be made is known as the 'make or buy' decision. Every finished product requires a series of components and parts. The decision facing managers is whether to make these parts themselves from raw materials, or to buy them from other specialist manufacturers. For example, when General Motors builds cars, should it make its own electrical switches, or should it buy them from a company which makes them? When Hewlett-Packard makes computers, should it manufacture its own semiconductors and hard disks, or buy them from specialist makers? The answer depends always on a variety of factors, but ultimately the decision is made on the basis of cheapness and convenience. If the company can make components more cheaply than it can buy them, and if setting up a separate production facility would not divert too many resources from the main task, then it may be wisest to make components. But if the cost of setting up such a facility would be too great, then buying in components is usually the best course of action. Computer companies buy in virtually all their major components such as chips and hard disks for precisely this reason.

INFRASTRUCTURAL DECISIONS
基础结构决策

Decisions about infrastructure are made with a view to supporting the main manufacturing structure. Some of the decisions that have to be made at this point include:

- *Human resource decisions*—how many staff will be required, and where will they be deployed? What skills will they need? These decisions should be made in close co-operation with the human resource management department.
- *Capital requirements*—how much investment is required to set up a production facility such as a factory, and to keep it running efficiently. Calculations such as profitability and rate of return on investment need to be made here (see Chapter 7), and these will require input from the finance department.
- *Quality control*—how will quality be assured and maintained? This involves the design of a quality control system as part of the manufacturing process. Input from the marketing department or function is an essential part of this, as quality is, initially at least, defined by customer needs (see below).
- *New products and new technologies*—manufacturing strategy has to plan for the future, of course, and this means the possible introduction of either new products or new and more efficient processes for making products. Research and development (see below) is carried out on a regular basis in order to forecast and introduce new products and new technologies, and this function too requires the allocation of resources.

MANUFACTURING SYSTEMS
制造系统

There is a huge variety of production systems, of course, as every product has different specifications and different companies may use different technologies to produce very similar products. There are, however, some basic tasks that are common to all production management. Every system has to be:

(1) designed, (2) set up and installed, (3) operated in order to make products, and (4) maintained so as to retain operating efficiency.

Design of the system follows on from the development of the manufacturing strategy and plan. The actual design of the system depends on what products are to be made and in what quantity. The design of the system brings together human and mechanical resources, labour and technology, and combines them in the most efficient and effective way.

Once designed, the system is then physically installed: the machinery is set up and tested and the workers rehearse the tasks required of them. Depending on whether the system is set up for job, batch or mass production (see below), it may be necessary to change the system from time to time in order to accommodate new products. In this case, management will try to use as many standard elements as possible, changing only what must be changed to accommodate new production. For example, if stamped metal products are being made, it will often be better to have a single machine which can be fitted with a number of different stamps which can be changed over between jobs, rather than needing to uninstall one machine and install a completely different one, as this will take longer and cost more.

During the actual process of production, management monitors input and output and checks to see that targets and schedules are being met, that the supply of materials and parts is unimpeded, and the finished goods are of the appropriate quality (see below for more on quality). Finally, production line machines require regular maintenance. Often production managers schedule regular maintenance periods, when production is stopped and machines are serviced, cleaned and checked to ensure that they are operating efficiently. Regular maintenance prolongs the life of machinery and ensures that the machines produce more goods, thus generating more revenue. However, some ongoing maintenance will also be essential, if only to deal with unexpected breakdowns.

Ideally, manufacturing systems are characterized by simplicity, repetition, and homogeneity. Simple systems are less costly to implement and less prone to failure. Repetition means that if the same tasks are done in sequence, practice means that tasks can be performed more quickly and more efficiently over time. This does not mean that work has to be repetitive and boring, nor does it mean that changes and improvements cannot be made; but unnecessary change should be avoided as it is costly and time-consuming. Any changes should be made with a view only to improving the system, and should be carefully planned in advance. Finally, homogeneity means that common elements and materials should be employed where possible. In cases where a production system switches from making one product to making another, the same machinery and components should be employed as far as possible. More is said on this under batch production, below.

JOB, BATCH AND MASS PRODUCTION　分批生产和大批量生产

In job production, each product is built to a particular specification. Very often products are specially ordered by customers: examples might include heavy machinery, large power generators, some kinds of precision instruments, specialist parts and so on. Job production is necessarily costly because not only does the business have to make the product, it also has to design both the product itself and the means by which it will be produced. Existing technology has to be reconfigured and adapted, and sometimes new technology has to be brought in.

Batch production involves production of limited quantities of identical items. For example, a company which makes moulded plastic products may receive an order for a few thousand plastic bottles of a particular shape and volume, or an electronics maker may be asked to produce several hundred switches of identical design. Sometimes these orders are one-offs, while in other cases the order might be repeated at some point in the future. However, the production run is limited, and when it is finished the production line must be reconfigured to make some other product (assuming marketing has found more orders to fill). Batch production is not as costly as job production because the production line only has to be set up once, regardless of the number of products to be made.

Mass production or line production involves continuous production of the same or very similar products on an ongoing basis. Soap powder, vodka and automobiles are all examples of continuous production lines which simply carry on producing the same standard product, sometimes for years at a time.

In actual production, the separation between job, batch and mass production is not absolute, and each system borrows elements from the other. Under the principle of homogeneity, above, job and batch production try to standardize tools and equipment as far as possible to avoid unnecessary costs. And increasingly, mass production has to be flexible enough to tailor products for different customer needs. This can be something as simple as allowing the same car production line to make cars of different colours, but more complex forms of what Japanese managers call 'mass customization' can be found as well.

EFFICIENCY AND EFFECTIVENESS
效率和效果

We discussed these two concepts in the opening chapter, but in production terms they have slightly more specific connotations. Effectiveness, for a production department, becomes a measure of how well the department is able to meet its targets in terms of producing the goods that customers need and putting them into the distribution chain so that customers are able to buy them. Efficiency becomes a measure of how cost-effective the department is: has it managed to achieve the maximum possible productivity from the inputs of human resources, technology and raw materials/parts? Two key issues in production efficiency are waste and time.

WASTE　废品

Early manufacturing businesses were highly inefficient, and large portions of raw materials and parts were wasted. The scientific management movement of the first decade of the twentieth century concentrating on reducing waste by standardizing work and ensuring that jobs and tasks were given exact specifications. Although scientific management has since been largely discredited, a number of its key ideas were incorporated into later management thinking, and the idea that waste is the enemy of efficiency is one of these.

Ideally, all the materials the business buys in, be they raw materials or parts, should be completely consumed and used to make finished products. This does not always happen: there are accidents, spillages, breakages and so on, and some materials are always lost. This is particularly the case in the food processing industry, for example, where problems such as contamination of the processing equipment with foreign (and potentially unhealthy) substances is a frequent cause of materials being wasted. That said, management can work to keep waste within tolerable limits. A food processing company might set itself a target of ensuring that no more than 5 per cent of the raw food it processes will be wasted, and the other 95 per cent will be made into finished products and sold. So long as it budgets for this and sticks to this target, the company can accept a limited amount of waste.

Waste becomes much more of an issue in service indus-tries, and as we shall see below, a certain loss of efficiency is sometimes necessary in order to achieve full service effective-ness. This rarely applies in the making of products, where effi-ciency and effectiveness are generally closely correlated.

TIME 时间

To the problem of the waste of materials must be added the problem of the waste of time. If a machine malfunctions and has to be shut down, or an employee does not turn up for work and there is no one there to operate the machine, then part or all of the production system must be shut down. When this happens, production time is wasted. Consider the following. A production system making soft drink bottles has an output of 3,000 bottles per hour. The company sells the bottles to customers at 20 cents a bottle. If the system has to be shut down for two hours be-cause a key piece of machinery has failed, then 6,000 bottles will not be made, with a loss in revenue of $1,200. What is more, other people who work on the same system are left stand-ing idle, but the company still has to pay their wages. That money and time are lost irrevocably; and in order to fulfil its or-der, the next job the company does will have to be delayed by two hours so that it can catch up on the first order. Customers may get annoyed and go elsewhere. The final loss could end up being far more than the initial $1,200.

时间就是金钱

The old saying that 'time is money' still applies in pro-duction departments. Writers on management, especially spe-cialists in marketing and human resources, sometime criticize production managers and engineers for their 'linear' thinking and old-fashioned approaches to problem-solving. But the prob-lems of production management are usually simple in their es-sence: how do we keep the system going, to deliver the right goods of the right quality to the right people at the right cost?

But remember: just because the problem appears simple, it does not mean the solution will be easy.

QUALITY 质量

Quality is free.
（Philip Crosby）

质量是免费的

Quality is one of the issues on which production managers spend a great deal of time and energy. Again, the basic problem is simple. Customers, through the marketing department, demand goods of a certain level of quality. If the production department cannot deliver goods that meet or exceed customer needs, then customers will be dissatisfied and will turn elsewhere.

Poor quality does not necessarily mean that a good is 'bad', although it can be that too. We as customers might reject a soft drink because it has unpleasant-looking sediment in the bottom of the bottle; this means the product was not made properly and may taste bad or even, in extreme cases, be dangerous. But we might also reject it because it is too sweet, or not sweet enough, and does not conform to what our tastes imagine a soft drink should be.

This brings us to one of the first principles of quality: ultimately, quality is what the customer says it is. It is not necessarily dependent on high standards or luxury, though it can be. The Rolls-Royce Silver Ghost and the Volkswagen Beetle were each, in their own way, high-quality automobiles; each met or exceeded customer expectations, the one for a top of the range luxury automobile, the other for a car that was cheap, affordable and reliable. As noted in the previous chapter, the marketing department plays a pivotal role in finding out what customers want and in defining the standards that the production department must meet.

ACHIEVING QUALITY 实现质量

For production, the challenge is then to meet the quality targets that have been established and to do so consistently. This means first, defining exactly how the product should be produced, drawing up a very detailed specification that describes the finished product and its components: a processed foodstuff would have a very exact list of ingredients, cooking times, materials to be used for packaging, temperature at which ingredients and finished product are to be stored, and so on. Second, it is necessary to ensure that the production system delivers the product to these specifications as consistently as possible.

There are, in essence, two ways of ensuring that only products of the right quality get to the customer. The first is through inspection, checking finished goods as they come off the production line and ensuring that they meet the specification. This can work when the volume of goods being produced is relatively low; there may then be time to stop and examine each one. But when hundreds of products are being made each hour, it simply is not feasible to examine every one for defects. And in some cases, physical examination is impossible; one can only check the quality of a tin of tomatoes by opening it, and this of course renders the tin unfit for sale. So in high-volume production, inspectors can only sample occasional items, and assume that the proportion of defects they find is on average correct across the board. This in turn means that some defective products are getting through to customers. Companies that use this system work to what they feel is an acceptable defect rate, say, one defect in every thousand products; if the inspectors find more defects than this, the company will look at the system again to find out what is going wrong, but otherwise will let the system be.

The second method is to literally 'build in' quality from

the beginning of the system, ensuring that the right products are made through system design. This is more expensive in terms of initial investment, but should result in less wastage, more satisfied customers and higher sales. Because a quality system should ultimately result in greater profitability, it is sometimes said that 'quality is free'; whatever management spends on getting quality will be made back several times over. The most famous system for building in quality is known as total quality management.

TOTAL QUALITY MANAGEMENT
全面质量管理

In the 1970s, so the story goes, an American computer maker ordered a batch of silicon microchips from a Japanese supplier and set what the Americans regarded as a very rigid requirement: the company would only accept one defective chip per one thousand ordered. When the first batch of ten thousand chips arrived, American managers were puzzled to find a small box containing a further ten chips. Unable to work out what these were for, they finally telephoned their opposite numbers in Japan. 'Oh', came the reply. 'Those are the ten defects you asked for.'

The story may be apocryphal, but it illustrates a point: Japanese firms, far from being satisfied with an acceptable defect rate, were pursuing a policy of 'zero defects' and aiming to completely eliminate error from the production process. The first attempts to design an error-free production process had begun at the Japanese carmaker Toyota in the 1930s, and continued after the Second World War when two Japanese engineers, Ohno Taiichi and Shingo Shigeo, developed the rudiments of total quality management. Other Japanese engineers, notably the scientist Ishikawa Kaoru, began to get involved and the practices developed at Toyota were gradually spread to other Japanese companies. Two American engineers, W. Edwards Deming and Joseph Juran, also became involved in the 1950s and 1960s. Both had, independently, developed systems for controlling quality, but had been unable to persuade American companies to listen to them. Prophets without honour in their own country, they found a ready audience in Japan. By the 1980s, Japanese companies were far exceeding many American companies in terms of quality products, and this was having serious consequences for American industry, particularly in areas like car production. Deming and Juran were 'discovered' by American management and along with a third engineer, Philip Crosby of the aircraft maker Martin, began to introduce concepts like total quality management and zero defects into Western thinking.

The essence of total quality management is that instead of inspecting for quality at the end of the production process, quality is managed at every stage of the process: from selection of raw materials through every element of design and manufacture. In many products, a mistake at any point can have serious consequences for later stages of manufacture: if the sole of a shoe is cut to the wrong size the upper will not fit, if a car's brake unit is wrongly made then the whole car becomes dangerous, and so on. This means too, that everyone in the company, management and workers, has to be conscious of quality and to make it a priority. Rather than having 'quality managers' who were solely responsibility for quality, in the words of Deming, 'quality is everyone's business'.

Deming, Juran and Crosby also argued that quality was an issue not only for production departments but for everyone in the organization, and urged that a 'quality philosophy' be adopted to ensure that the whole company made quality a priority. It was not acceptable that marketing and production should argue over what quality really meant, or that the two departments should have to unite against a finance department wanting to reduce quality so as to cut costs. Quality, they said, must be a compa-ny-wide issue, and everyone should agree on quality targets and how to meet them.

CONTINUOUS IMPROVEMENT
持续改进

Even under total quality management and a policy of zero defects, it is recognized that some problems will still occur. Moreover, even if quality targets are achieved absolutely, be-cause the customer defines the nature of quality, the targets themselves will be constantly moving. A 'perfect' bicycle, free of defects and giving full customer satisfaction, is built, and this suffices for the needs of the market for the moment. But in a few months or a few years, the market will change. People will want longer handlebars, or brake levers closer to the centre of the bars, or thicker and wider tyres for off-road use. The manufacturer has to respond to this.

Continuous improvement is another term derived from Japa-nese management (the Japanese term is *kaizen*), particularly from Toyota. Like total quality management, continuous im-provement is a management philosophy which, it is argued, everyone in the organization needs to embrace. Even if customer requirements are currently being met, the future must always be considered. Continuous improvement allows the steady improve-ment of the quality of products with minimal disruption to pro-duction systems.

PRODUCTION FLOWS AND SUPPLY
CHAINS　生产流动和供应链

From total quality management there also evolved a view of production not so much as a series of processes but as a single continuous process or 'flow', starting with raw materials and parts and ending with the finished goods. Likewise there developed the notion of the supply chain, which sees raw materials being produced, perhaps being manufactured at a first stage as parts or components, then bought by the primary manufacturer who creates finished goods, which are then shipped through distributors to retailers and finally to customers.

Compare this integrated idea of the supply chain to Michael Porter's value chain (Porter 1980). (Figure 6. 1 shows this comparison in more detail.) It can be seen that the two are closely related. Both see a continuous flow from supplier to customer. The supply chain concept shows how the flow is managed; the value chain concept shows how the flow acts to add value for the customer or consumer. In recent years, advances in communications technology have made full integrated supply chain management possible. Increasingly, manufacturing companies are no longer just buying from suppliers and selling on to distributors or customers. They are working in partnership with suppliers, distributors and retailers to manage the whole process in an integrated way, to both increase productivity and profits and to add further value for customers.

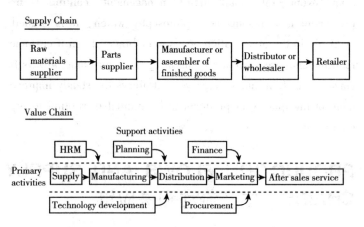

Figure 6. 1   Supply chains and value chains

GLOBAL FLOWS 全球流动

Increasingly, the production of sophisticated goods such as cars and computers is taking place all around the world, as companies seek cheaper and more efficient means of production. In some industries, especially those such as electronics where prices may be stable or falling, keeping production costs low is a major competitive strategy. Planners are constantly looking for locations where advantages can be gained. Not only are parts and raw materials sourced, quite literally, from all over the world, but even individual stages of production may be scattered widely. The production of a single microprocessor, for example, might take several stages from the production of the initial silicon wafer to the finished and tested product, and each of those stages might be carried out in a different country, the chip migrating from Singapore to Brazil to France to the United States as each stage in the chain is passed.

Global production of this kind requires very detailed planning and also strong communications links so that managers can have access to knowledge about the current state of production, any problems that may be arising and so on, at any time and anywhere in the world. Global production systems are also rendered more complex by different work cultures that may exist at different points in the system. A good understanding of the role played by knowledge (see Chapter 8) and culture (see Chapter 9) is essential for managing these systems.

JUST IN TIME 实时生产方式

Another concept to come out of the Japanese experience is the idea of 'just-in-time' (JIT) ordering and supply. The practice of JIT was again developed at Toyota, concurrently with total quality management. JIT means that companies order parts and materials when they need them, so that rather than holding large stocks of parts and materials in advance (which ties up warehouse space and capital), the parts and materials are only ordered and paid for as they are actually used or consumed. JIT can be turned around the other way, as well, with the company only making and shipping goods when customers order them. Retailers also use just-in-time ordering systems to reduce the volume of stock they have to hold in warehouses.

JIT has been proven to work, and has many cost and efficiency advantages. However, for it to work, communications between the company and its suppliers and customers up and down the supply chain have to be very good indeed. Delays in processing or transmitting orders can mean that ready stocks of parts, materials or goods will run out and the entire system will then slow or halt. Some large businesses will insist on controlling the location of their suppliers; the Vauxhall works at Luton in Britain (part of General Motors), for example, once required many of its key suppliers to establish their own factories and workshops directly outside Vauxhall's own front gate, so as to improve communications and limit transport times. Other car companies use more geographically distributed networks of suppliers.

Another aspect of JIT is that industrial relations also need to be good. A single strike or work stoppage can again block the whole system. In 2000, a strike at three main suppliers to General Motors, which uses a global JIT system, resulted in other production facilities quickly running out of necessary parts. Stopping work at these factories meant further slowdowns elsewhere, and within a week more than 200 General Motors production facilities world-wide had either had to stop work or were running at drastically reduced capacity. JIT shows once again the importance of harmony and coordination, ensuring that all elements of the organization—and indeed all elements of the entire supply chain—are working closely together.

BUSINESS PROCESS RE-ENGINEER-ING　业务流程再造

When speaking of production flows, a word should also be said about business process re-engineering (BPR), a popular management 'fad' of the early 1990s. In a fashion not unlike the early scientific management, though using much more sophisticated methods and information technology, BPR broke production down into minutely detailed tasks, examined each to see how it could be performed most efficiently, and then pulled the tasks back together again to create 'flows' of work from one end of the organization to the other, from parts and materials to finished goods. In this second stage, tasks that were not considered essential to the flow were eliminated, and attention focused on making the flow as smooth and efficient as possible.

BPR was seen as the salvation of business, especially American business, by many, but there were some spectacular abuses of the idea. Over-enthusiastic managers and consultants did not just eliminate waste and unnecessary tasks but, in some cases, actually destroyed working parts of their organizations and ended up by rendering them less efficient and effective than before. Two of the leading thinkers on BPR, Thomas Davenport and Michael Hammer, have strongly criticized such abuses and have pointed out that BPR does have its limits; it is a useful tool, but it is not a panacea.

BPR did do several useful things. It reinforced the product flow concept, and it developed very useful tools such as flowcharts for studying these. It also strengthened the idea of task efficiency: where many proponents went wrong was in failing to recognize the need for effectiveness as well. A business organization is of course more than the sum of its parts, but the parts

do need to be got right. BPR showed how a single badly designed or badly performed task or process can cause a bottle-
neck that weakens the entire system, and reinforced the need
for careful system design.

RESEARCH AND DEVELOPMENT
研究与开发

　　Research and development (R&D) properly comes before
production, and will in fact be discussed in more detail in the
chapter on knowledge (see Chapter 8). Most companies of any
size will have a separate R&D department, the primary function
of which is to create new knowledge which can be turned into
either new products or new and better processes for making
products.

　　Research and development is the focus for innovation in
any business, but it is not the sole source of innovation. Innovation can, and should, come from anywhere in the company.
However, a formal R&D department can do things that other
managers and workers do not have time or resources to do, like
pioneering new basic technologies and testing new ideas in detail. To this end R&D also works closely with marketing, carrying out much of the detailed testing of new products and product
features. Some organizations link their R&D function closely to
marketing, others see it as part of the overall production department, and still others keep it independent of both, with the director of R&D sometimes reporting directly to the chairman or
chief executive.

　　The basic aim of R&D is to create knowledge, and then
find ways for knowledge to be usefully employed. While the
R&D department is the focus of this activity, it is worth repeat-
ing that other managers and employees need to be involved as
well.

PRODUCING SERVICES　生产服务

The bulk of this chapter has dealt with the production of physical, tangible products, whether produced one at a time or in tens of thousands on a production line. However, most of the comments above also apply to services, with some adaptation. The same kinds of structural and infrastructural decisions have to be made when planning; the same criteria of efficiency and effectiveness apply; quality is equally important; the concept of flow can be applied to services in very much the same way as to tangible products.

However, services do have some differences. In Chapter 5 on marketing we referred to some of these differences, and it is worth reminding ourselves again of the two most important of these differences and noting their consequences for the production of services.

First, services cannot be stored. Services are consumed as they are produced; it is not possible to keep a stockpile of services ready to be offered when consumers want them. It is possible to keep stocks of goods that consumers need as part of the services, such as hamburger patties or car parts, but these are not the same as the service itself. This has obvious implications for efficiency. It is at least theoretically possible to configure a production line so it runs at 100 per cent efficiency, with no wasted time or materials, and this is indeed the standard to which production managers often aspire. But, as we noted in Chapter 5, it is not possible to run a restaurant so that its full seating capacity is used 100 per cent of the time; for if this should be the case, there will almost certainly be consequences for customer satisfaction. The best that services production people can do is try to plan for peak times and minimize inefficiency, while at the same time focusing on effectiveness and delivering the best possible service.

Second, the customer is part of the service; as services

marketers sometimes say, 'the customer is part of the factory'. A service has to be consumed as well as delivered, and the interaction between customer and service provider is an important part of the service. This in turn has implications for quality, which will tend to be more subjective and will depend in part on that interaction and how successful it is. Indeed, the same restaurant customer and the same waiter can create two quite different interactions at different times; one day the waiter may be friendly and pleasant, the next day surly and disgruntled, or the customer may enjoy the food one day and dislike it the next. It is difficult to inspect quality at the end of the service process, and the imperative to build as much quality as possible into the process becomes very strong. Finally, services managers must plan for the possibility of service failure and develop procedures for recovery from failure in order to ensure customers are happy once more.

摘要

● 生产的职能是生产消费者需要的产品。

● 生产与其他的各项职能相互协调，包括市场营销、人力资源、财务和研发。

● 生产可以看作一系列的流程，从进入公司的原材料和货物到沿着供应链用它们生产出成品。

● 生产的目标是讲求效率和效益，在合适的时间，以公司能够盈利的成本生产合适的商品。

● 质量是生产的本质特征，质量的管理就是负责生产部门中的每个人，实际上可以是公司的每个人的责任。

SUGGESTIONS FOR FURTHER READING
延伸阅读

Deming, W. E. *Out of the Crisis*, Cambridge, MA: MIT Center for Advanced Engineering Study, 1986.

One of the best books ever written about making things, talking about quality and much else besides. See also Andrea

Gabor's biography of Deming, The Man Who Discovered Quality (*New York*: *Times Books*, 1990), *and the key works of the other two quality gurus*, *Joseph Juran's* Juran on Leadership for Quality: An Executive Handbook (*New York*: *The Free Press*, 1989) *and Philip Crosby's* Quality is Free: The Art of Making Quality Certain (*New York*: *McGraw-Hill*, 1979).

Hill, T. , *The Strategy Quest*, London: Prentice Hall, 1994.

Despite its title, this book is actually a novel about how to focus and reorient a manufacturing system and align it with other parts of the organization. It is light and easy to read for beginners, but has some very powerful themes and ideas nonetheless.

Ohno, Taiichi, *Toyota Production System*, Cambridge, MA: Productivity Press, 1988.

A description of the world-famous Toyota system of manufacturing, by one of the people most closely involved with that system. For an outsider's view of the same, see J. P. Womack, D. T. Jones and D. Roos, The Machine That Changed the World (*New York*: *Macmillan*, 1990).

FINANCE
财　务

The objects of a financier are, then, to secure an ample revenue; to impose it with judgment and equality; to employ it economically; and, when necessity obliges him to make use of credit, to secure its foundations in that instance, and for ever, by the clearness and candor of his proceedings, the exactness of his calculations, and the solidity of his funds.

（Edmund Burke）

财务是新的目标：确保充足的收入，公平合理地征税，并经济地使用。

——埃德蒙·伯克

Corporate finance is, or can be, a very complex subject. The methods of calculation used in reporting and control procedures are often very complex, as are the financial instruments that financial managers use. This is so much the case that financial managers are increasingly being trained quite separately from other managers, and financial management is becoming seen in academic circles as a discipline in its own right.

But although the instruments and methods are complex, the basics of corporate finance are actually very simple. The corporate finance function must accomplish three sets of tasks: management accounting, the allocation of resources within the business; financial accounting, the presentation of financial data for those outside the company; and treasury, the actual management of money including receiving income and disbursing funds. How businesses accomplish these three functions can vary, and each has a number of subordinate functions; but these are, in essence, what corporate finance does. This chapter focuses on understanding those basic functions and processes; for more information on the tools of corporate finance, consult the suggestions for further reading at the end of the chapter.

Although corporate finance is taught very much as a specialist sub-discipline within management, this does not mean that finance is in some way 'separate' from the rest of business. At the topmost level, the chief financial officer or finance director is a key member of the board of directors and has an important say in strategy and decision-making in many fields; increasingly, the CFO is being regarded as the most important person on the board after the chief executive officer. At lower levels, the finance department provides resources and information that the rest of the company needs if it is to function effectively. And, equally importantly, the finance department is one of the focal points of liaison between those people and organizations outside the business that provide its capital, the shareholders and debtholders.

DEFINITIONS　定义

Accounting　Accounting at its simplest level is keeping　会计
track of the movement and location of money. It is through accounts that companies know how much money they have, how much they are spending and earning. Analysis of accounts gives critical information such as profitability (how much money is the company making), gross expenditure (how much is it spending) and so on. Managers use accounts rather as drivers or pilots use maps, to tell them where they are at any given point in time and where they can go next.

预算

Budgeting　Budgeting is a form of planning that specifies how much money will be allocated to a particular activity over a given period of time. Financial managers usually prepare overall budgets which state how much money the company will spend on operating expenses, both ordinary costs and costs for special products over a period of time, typically a year. There are two ways of preparing an overall budget; either individual departments, divisions, business units and so on prepare their own budgets for their own activities and then the finance department aggregates these into an overall budget; or the finance department prepares a framework budget and tells the various other departments and divisions how much money they can spend, leaving each to allocate money more precisely as they see fit.

资本

Capital　In finance terms, capital is money put into the business. Most commonly, capital is raised in one of three ways: (1) by borrowing money directly from banks or other institutions, (2) by the sale of bonds, financial instruments which are sold to investors and then bought back (or 're-deemed') at a specified date in the future, or (3) through the sale of shares, which give investors part ownership in the corporation and the right to a share of its profits (if any).

股东

Shareholder　A shareholder is a person who has purchased a share in the business as above. In return for their money, shareholders are given 'equity', a stake in the business and its profits. Formerly shareholders were also theoretically liable for a company's debts as well, and if a company went bankrupt and its debts totalled more than its assets and the equity issued to shareholders, then debtors could attempt to recover money from the shareholders. Today, virtually all companies, even very small ones, operate on the principle of limited liability, meaning that shareholders are not responsible for debts incurred by the company. However, if the company does go bankrupt, the shareholders will probably lose part or all of the money they have invested.

Debtholder　A debtholder is anyone who lends money 债权人
directly to a business, such as a bank, or anyone holding any
other debt instrument such as mortgage on property owned by
the business. Owners of bonds are also considered to be debtholders, as the ownership of bonds signifies that the person has
invested money in the company which is to be paid back; there
is no transfer of equity involved.

MANAGEMENT ACCOUNTING
管理会计

The management accounting function of the business has
two principal tasks: first, planning and allocating financial resources, and second, ensuring that resources once allocated are
used in an appropriate and effective manner. Management accounting is also involved in various special decisions such as developing new products, new investments in technology, entering
new markets and the like. At the heart of management accounting lies the need for information, by all parts of the organization, about how much money is being made, how much spent,
and how this affects future plans and prospects.

The two key figures that management accounting looks at
are *costs* and *income*, or revenue. Costs include everything that
the business will spend in order to operate: wages, raw materials, stationery and computer peripherals, machinery and equipment, rent for premises, insurance, electricity, travel costs for
employees, maintenance and so on. Costs are sometimes divided into direct costs, those which are directly incurred in the
production of products (primarily wages and materials) and in-
direct costs, those which are incurred by the organization regardless of what it is making and selling, such as insurance,
rent and electricity bills.

Another form of cost which needs to be considered is depreciation, effectively meaning the wear and tear on machinery and equipment which occurs with use. If a computerized lathe is purchased for $50,000 and can be expected to last for five years before needing to be replaced, then the lathe is said to depreciate at a rate of $10,000 a year. Its value after a year of use will be $40,000, after two years $30,000 and so on. Although no money is actually spent on replacing the lathe during this time, the reduction in value is nonetheless regarded technically as a cost.

Income is what the company earns, primarily but not exclusively through the sale of products and services to customers. Other means of making income might include the sale of redundant machinery, buildings or premises, or contracting the right to make the company's products to another company under a licensing agreement (for example, a maker of electrical generators in the USA might allow a South Korean company to make the same product under licence, paying the American company an annual fee for doing so).

The comparison of income to costs yields a ratio known as income over expenditure. If income is $1 million in the course of a year, and costs are $500,000, then the income over expenditure ratio is said to be 2:1. However, another factor then has to be determined, namely whether there are any other charges the company must pay out of its income. The most important of these are repayment of debts and payment of taxes—companies are not allowed to declare tax as a cost—and this will reduce the amount of money available. If in the example above the company then pays $250,000 in tax (unlikely, but a simplification for our purposes), the net income, after taxes, would be $750,000. This yields a ratio known as profitability or profit to loss, which is net income (total income less tax and other charges) compared to costs. In the above example, the profit to loss ratio would be 1.5:1. Calculating a little further, we see that the company is then left with $250,000 in profits ($1 million income, less $500,000 in costs, less $250,000 in taxes).

When planning and allocating resources, management accounting estimates overall costs and income from all the various activities of the business, and builds up a composite forecast of what the year (or two years, or three, whatever the reporting period might be) ahead might hold. If it looks like income will exceed costs by a reasonable margin, well and good; the company will have a financial surplus, which it can reinvest in operations, pay out as dividends to shareholders or some combination of the two, as the board of directors decides. If income and costs will be closely matched, or costs will exceed income, then other measures may need to be taken. A company can run at a loss—though more capital may need to be raised to cover the loss—for a time, but not indefinitely.

The outcome of this planning process has an effect on almost everything the company does. The amount of money the company is forecast to make—or lose—in the coming year determines how much the business can afford to spend on developing new products or investing in new technology. If the results are unsatisfactory, then managers will have to look at other issues. Can costs be saved, by reducing overheads or wages? Can the price of its goods and services be raised? Ideally, of course, these are not decisions that are made only when a crisis point is reached; rather, financial managers and managers of other departments should be in constant touch, looking at ways of increasing revenue and ensuring costs are at an optimum level. This should not be a case of the finance department telling the other departments what to do; rather, all departments should work together to interpret what the financial forecasts might mean.

Once this is done, budgets are then prepared, usually on an annual basis, for each department and business unit. This involves detailed planning of expenditure over the coming year, not forgetting an allowance for unforeseen events or emergencies. The latter is known as contingency planning. One of the key activities of the finance department is assessing risk: that is, what might happen to throw plans off their course, and if they do go off course, what are the financial implications? The company tries to anticipate what risks it is running and anticipate future unplanned events, and then develop alternative plans which can be put into place if such an event occurs. For example, if a key piece of equipment breaks down and must be replaced, there may be a contingency plan for such an event, with costs savings then being made elsewhere.

Finally, there is the monitoring of expenditure and income, the activity most of us think of first when we think of accounting. All expenditure and income, no matter where in the business, must be recorded and reported to management accounting. If this does not happen, then there is a risk that the final figures for the year will be inaccurate and the company's picture of its financial performance will not be a true one. There is also a risk that, if the transfer of money is not recorded, money may actually be getting lost—or worse, stolen. The problem of accounts not reflecting an accurate picture of performance and allowing corrupt individuals to steal from the company has been highlighted in the past few years by a series of accounting scandals in the USA and around the world, notably Enron.

At the end of the reporting period, management accounting totals income, profit and costs and reports on financial performance to the board. At this point the information becomes the province of the second finance function, financial accounting. Note that in many companies, management accounting and financial accounting are actually done by the same people and have many areas of overlap; nevertheless the two activities have separate purposes, and are treated separately here.

FINANCIAL ACCOUNTING　财务会计

Whereas management accounting looks inside the company, financial accounting looks outside and presents factual information about the company to shareholders, debtholders, regulatory bodies and government tax authorities, all of whom will require such information on at least an annual basis, and sometimes more often than that. The key document which financial accounting prepares is the financial statement, which shows profit and loss for the past year, forecasts profit and loss for the coming year, and spells out in detail what money will be spent on and how revenue will be distributed between shareholders, debtholders and reinvestment in the company.

These annual statements will need to be supplemented by more frequent reports and forecasts. Major shareholders in particular will want frequent information. If the company's shares are traded on a stock market (see below), then markets too will want reports, especially if the company's fortunes look like changing. An example of such a report is the profit warning, which most companies are required to issue if their shares are traded publicly. If a company has issued an annual forecast that its profits for the period to come will be a certain amount, say $10 million, and then if part way through the period managers find that profits will only be $5 million, they are duty bound to report this publicly. Failure can lead in many jurisdictions to fines being imposed by the market or other regulators, and will also anger shareholders.

One of the central issues in management accounting is the notion of transparency. This means that the company's internal financial workings must be visible and understandable to the outside world, and shareholders and regulators—at least—must be able to see clearly that management is running the company efficiently and effectively and is not behaving dishonestly. Regular reporting—and stringent penalties for false reporting—are one measure which aims to achieve transparency. Recent legislation in the USA, the Sarbanes-Oxley Act which passed through Congress in 2002, now requires directors to sign all financial statements guaranteeing that they are accurate; if it later transpires that the statements are not accurate and if criminal intent is proved, then directors can face fines and prison terms.

Another method of ensuring transparency is through auditing. All accounts and financial statements are double-checked by another party before being issued. Many businesses have internal auditors who in effect check the work of other members of the finance department. Large corporations also have an audit committee, often chaired by a non-executive director, which checks final financial statements and reports directly to the board. Finally, companies are required by law almost everywhere to submit all their accounts and records to an independent auditor, usually a chartered accountant or accounting firm, who checks for accuracy. The primary purpose of the independent auditor is to ensure that there has been no criminal activity, such as theft of money or concealing funds to avoid paying taxes, but auditors may also be asked to advise on accounting practices and reporting more generally as well.

One of the problems which frequently arises in this field is when businesses, especially those that are performing badly, become reluctant to disclose information which shows management in a negative light. Or they will take various measures to camouflage bad news; profit warnings, for example, may blame external factors for reduced profits and then claim the problem is outside the control of management. The SARS epidemic in 2003 did indeed affect the profits of airlines and travel companies, but claims by booksellers and clothing retailers that their profits had been affected were regarded by markets in a more dubious light. What, investors asked, was really going on in these firms? Transparency is often seen as something to be complied with grudgingly and only to the letter of the law in order to avoid penalties. In fact, transparency usually tends to work to the benefit of the business and its managers. 'Coming clean' with shareholders and debtholders is nearly always the best policy, especially if potential problems are warned about early enough for preventive measures to be taken. Shareholders and debtholders respect good, honest managers; they dislike and distrust those that they think are being less than fully honest.

The reason why shareholders and debtholders behave in this way, of course, is because they have given the business their money, and as long as shareholders hold equity or debtholders have made loans or bought bonds, then the business and its managers have custody of that money. They have a moral and legal responsibility to use that money wisely and return it, with profits, to the debtholders and to pay a portion of their net profits to shareholders.

The rules that govern this moral and legal responsibility are known as *corporate governance*. On one level, corporate governance spells out the legal rules by which managers must abide. On another level, however, it reminds managers that they do not own the businesses that they run, not unless they themselves own large numbers of shares. Otherwise, they are merely stewards or custodians, duty bound to manage the company to the best of their ability for the real owners, and to render full and frank accounts of their work when requested.

This may seem self-evident. But it is worth reminding ourselves why these rules are in place. A hundred years ago, American business was largely controlled by a few large, monopolistic businesses, sometimes known as trusts. These large corporations were highly secretive, rendered no accounts and did not give out information to shareholders or government. Inside companies like Standard Oil, a handful of senior managers controlled tens of billions of dollars, and there was no way of knowing whether they were using this money in a lawful or ethical manner. Nor were there laws to compel transparency such as we have now. When government did hold inquiries into the conduct of these organizations and summoned directors and senior managers to appear, the latter refused to answer or lied. John

D. Rockefeller, chairman of Standard Oil, repeatedly told a Congressional committee that he did not know how much oil his company refined and shipped or how much money it made. (Another director told the same committee that he 'did not know' what business was transacted at a certain address in New York city; the address was Standard Oil's own head office.) And yet records did exist, as was later discovered. It took a major campaign by radical journalists and liberal politicians to force a change in the law so that these big corporations had to come out into the open, and it was then found that many were badly and corruptly managed. We may tell ourselves that a century has passed and society has moved on, but the examples of Enron, Global Crossing, WorldCom and others show that corruption and mismanagement remain a possibility.

TREASURY　财务部

The treasury function actually handles money itself. It receives income and channels it to the appropriate destinations, such as bank accounts, and it handles disbursements. It issues shares, oversees the placing of these in stock markets where they can be sold to shareholders, and takes receipt of funds raised. It takes in money lent by debtors and received through the sale of bonds.

The treasury function also ensures that the money received, from whatever source, is used as efficiently as possible. If money is held in banks, the treasury function looks to get the best rate of interest possible, swapping money around from one account to another in search of the best deal. When millions of dollars are being held in bank accounts, even a tiny difference in interest rates can make a great deal of difference in terms of revenue.

For companies operating across national boundaries, there is also the need to handle foreign currency transactions. An

American company with an operating unit in Germany, for example, will receive income in Germany in the form of euros. Some of these euros will be used to pay costs and reinvest in Germany, but it may still be necessary to 'repatriate' some of these euros to America. What then should be done? Banks in America will allow the company to open a euro account, but the euros cannot be spent in America. In order to do so, the money will need to be exchanged into dollars, and this incurs costs. And, since the early 1970s, the major international currencies have floated against each other: that is, their values have been determined by international currency markets, where dealers set prices according to the perceived strength and weakness of each economy. Financial managers dealing across boundaries have to keep a close eye on currency movements. If on Monday the euro is worth 98 cents US, and on Tuesday rises to 99 cents US, the consequences for a company transferring 100 million euros are considerable; the euros are worth a million dollars less on Tuesday than they would have been on Monday. Sometimes companies will choose to hold onto their foreign currency for as long as they can, seeking a favourable exchange rate, but this is not always possible.

Two issues that further concern the treasury function are how many shares to issue and how much money to borrow. The issuing of shares requires a calculation of the value of the company and whether the issuing of further shares will harm the interests of existing shareholders. The calculation can be made quite simply. Suppose a company is valued at $1 million dollars. This is the money that would, in theory, be yielded if the company sold all of its assets and turned them into cash, including all its equipment and premises, any products in stock, outstanding contracts and the like, and paid off all its debts. The company has 100,000 outstanding shares. Each shareholder thus has $10 of equity for each share he or she holds (this is not necessarily related to the price the shares sell for, we will come onto this in a moment). Now suppose the company wishes to raise more money and decides to issue a further 100,000 shares. As the company is only worth $1 million, this means that with 200,000 outstanding shares, each shareholder would only have $5 per share. Not surprisingly, existing shareholders would object to this, and might try to block the new issue or would sell their shares before it took place. This reduction in the value of individual shares by issuing new shares is known as dilution. However, if the company value were to double to $2 million, it might be able to make a persuasive case for issuing new shares, especially if it offered them to existing shareholders at a cheaper price, and thus avoided dilution. Dilution becomes less of an issue if the company's share price is higher than the asset value of each share (the difference will be explained below), then the shares will be in demand and can be sold profitably by current shareholders.

As to how much debt the company should take on, opinions vary. Perhaps surprisingly, it is not always considered desirable for a company to be debt-free; it may be that the company can use its assets more effectively by borrowing against them. The ratio of debt to the value of the company is known as gearing; for example, if a company worth $100 million has debts of $40 million, it is said to be geared at 40 per cent. Generally, shareholders start to worry if gearing goes above 50 or 60 per cent, as the company will then be paying out large sums in interest which will have a negative effect on net profits, and the high level of debt will also reduce the overall value of the company. Gearing must not be allowed to reach 100 per cent, because if debts exceed assets the company is then deemed to be insolvent and no longer viable. In many jurisdictions it is illegal to trade while insolvent, and companies that reach this position can be broken up or dissolved. A second choice then concerns how to raise the money, through loans or by issuing bonds.

MONEY MARKETS　资金市场

Loans are negotiated directly with banks and other lenders (sometimes, companies will lend money to each other, without the need to go to a bank), but shares and bonds are sold in what are known as money markets. There are an increasing variety of these, dealing with ever more complex financial instruments, but as space is limited we will stick to the two most basic and common money markets, the stock market and the bond market. There are markets in everything from foreign currency to futures (markets for goods which have not yet been produced but will be produced in future) to hedge instruments (bets againstcertain events coming to pass) and many more, but these are not 'basic' to corporate finance.

Stock markets are where shares are sold. Companies wishing to issue equity make what is known as a placement, issuing shares and then placing these with a broker who in turn sells them on commission to investors. Investors come in several different forms. Private investors are individuals who buy for themselves, while institutional investors are large organizations such as pension funds and insurance companies who buy shares in order to earn money for their own business purposes. Income investors are those who buy shares in order to make money from dividends, portions of the company's net profit which are paid out annually to shareholders, while growth investors are primarily concerned with seeing the value of their shares grow so that they can sell them on at a profit. In general, institutional investors are more interested in income while private investors are more interested in growth, but there are plenty of exceptions to both rules.

Once shares have been issued, of course, the shareholder is perfectly free to sell his or her shares to someone else. The company that issued the shares cannot control either the sale itself or the price for which the shares are sold; the shares, once issued and paid for, are the property of the shareholders, who can do with them as they see fit. Companies by and large prefer to see their shareholders keep their shares rather than sell them, as it makes it possible to build up long-term relationships with shareholders. Also, if shares are sold, there is a risk that they will be sold to a rival company. The practice of takeovers, buying up the shares of competitors and then incorporating the business into that of the buyer or closing it down altogether, is a common competitive tactic.

Companies also like to see the price of their shares high, in part because it discourages rivals from buying their shares, and in part because if the price at which the shares trade is higher than the asset value, then there are opportunities to issue more shares with less risk of dilution. The difference between the market value of a share and its equity value is simply the difference between what people are willing to pay for a share and what the share represents in terms of a proportion of the company's equity. In the example above we talked about a company valued at $1 million, with 100,000 shares. These have an equity value of $10 each. However, if the company is deemed to be well managed and has good prospects for growth, investors may decide to buy shares in it now. There develops a competition for the shares, with those who currently own them charging whatever buyers are willing to pay; the price could rise to $12, $15 or even $20 depending on how confident investors are feeling. During the late 1990s, e-commerce companies known colloquially as dotcoms saw the market value of their shares rise to many times that of their actual asset value; companies whose assets were valued at only a few hundred thousand dollars saw the total market value of their shares rise to tens of millions of dollars, or more. Eventually, the market realized that the promises of growth were not going to come true, and the value of the shares crashed to nearly nothing.

Investors react quickly to news of either good fortune or

bad fortune. We come back here to the issue of transparency. Even if a company has done nothing wrong, even a whisper that it might have done something wrong will see investors sell shares rapidly and cause the share price to plunge. Good, transparent communications with shareholders are essential if the value of the shares is to hold up.

Bond markets are somewhat simpler. Although there is a bewildering variety of different types of bonds, most have a few simple features in common. The bondholder buys bonds, and the company is then free to use the money as it sees fit. In exchange, the company promises to redeem the bond, i. e. buy it back, at a specified date in the future, paying the bondholder a premium over and above what he or she purchased the bond for. Income on bonds is usually lower than for stocks, often only 2 – 4 per cent a year, but bonds are also seen as less risky because their value does not fluctuate. In order to successfully issue bonds, however, the company must be confident that it will have the money to redeem the bonds on the date specified.

摘要

● 财务的职能是管理企业中资金的流动，并负责报告和控制。

● 财务资源必须通过管理会计做好计划、预测和预算工作。

● 公司财务状况的报表需要通过财务会计准备。

● 公司的资金和负债由财务部管理。

● 在所有的财务管理中，沟通联络和透明度是最本质的要求，以便确保最准确的信息以及对法律和道德标准的遵守。

SUGGESTIONS FOR FURTHER READING
延伸阅读

Brealey, R. A. and Myers, S. C. , *Principles of Corporate Finance*, New York: McGraw-Hill, 5th edn, 1996.

A textbook for students, which goes into many of the tools and methods of financial management in great detail; strongly recommended. The introductory chapters treat key themes and are worth reading in any case.

Eiteman, D. K. , Stonehill, A. I, and Moffett, M. H. , *Multinational Business Finance*, Reading, MA: Addison-Wesley, 7th edn, 1995.

A clear and useful book, whose opening chapter gives a good introduction to the main issues of international financial management.

Giddy, I. H. , *Global Financial Markets*, Lexington, MA: D. C. Heath, 1994.

Good and clear, but the reader should be warned that there have been considerable changes in some of these markets since this book was written.

Heffernan, S. A. and Sinclair, P. J. N. , *Modern International Economics*, Oxford: Blackwell, 1990.

Technical in places, but the chapters on exchange rates and government economic policy are good and clear.

Smith, C. W. , Smithson, C. W. and Sykes, Wilford, D. , *Managing Financial Risk*, New York: Irwin, 1995.

This is still one of the best books on this subject, and the opening chapter is an excellent and clear introduction to the main issues.

8

KNOWLEDGE

知　　识

Capital is useless without knowledge.

（Milan Zeleny）

没有知识的资本是毫无用处的。

——米兰·季林尼

The importance of knowledge in business organizations has been recognized for some time. The first understanding of the role played by knowledge comes in the writings of the classical economists of the eighteenth and nineteenth centuries, especially the English economist Nassau Senior, who pointed out that workers do not just apply physical labour to their tasks, but also skills—i. e. their personal knowledge and experience of carrying out these tasks—and this has a bearing on how well the task is carried out. Karl Marx went still further and pointed out that work did not have to be physical labour at all, but could also be the 'mental labour' carried out by scientists, engineers and other thinkers. A few years after Marx, the British economist Alfred Marshall noted how mechanization was increasing the importance of 'mental labour' by requiring even ordinary workers to have more and more knowledge in order to work effectively.

However, it was not until the late 1980s and early 1990s that theorists began to think in specific terms about the role of knowledge in business. Some conceived of knowledge as a kind of catalyst, necessary in order to make capital and labour productive. Others thought of knowledge as a form of capital in its own right, a factor of production (see Chapter 6). Theories are still being developed in this new field, but most people are now aware of the importance of knowledge in business. A new sub-discipline of knowledge, 'knowledge management', has been created and a body of literature has been established and is accumulating rapidly.

Knowledge is critical to businesses in many ways. Knowledge of the market is vital to understanding what customers want, and whether and how the company can provide for their needs. Knowledge of technology is necessary to make the production process efficient; knowledge of people and human motivation is necessary to focus the efforts of the company on meeting its goals; knowledge of financial instruments and accounting methods is necessary to manage capital effectively. Few areas of business are not in some way affected by knowledge.

But, beyond passively accepting that knowledge is important and all around them, managers can also actively use knowledge to make the business more innovative, competitive and successful. One of the primary effects of the revolution in information technology in the 1980s has been to make access to knowledge, all kinds of knowledge, much more widespread around the world. The competitive advantage that new knowledge gives now does not last for long, meaning that it is important that businesses and managers create new knowledge on a continuous basis. In 1989, the Dutch writer Arie de Geus, formerly a senior manager with the oil company Royal Dutch/Shell, wrote in *Harvard Business Review* that in the future, a company's only sustainable competitive advantage may be its ability to learn. With that statement, the age of knowledge in management had definitively arrived.

DEFINITIONS　定义

　　Data　Data are 'facts', things that we see or hear or otherwise take in through our senses. Data can be columns of numbers in a spreadsheet or table in a book, or simple statements of fact such as 'The company made a profit last year of $3.2 million.' Sometimes a distinction is made between 'hard' data, usually facts expressed as numbers and easily proven to be true or false, and 'soft data', more general sensory impressions such as seeing that a traffic light has changed from green to red.

数据

　　Information　Information is conveyed to people by means of data. When we read, hear or see data, we interpret them in light of our own prior knowledge. Reading in a company annual report that 'The company made a profit last year of $3.2 million', informs us that the company is profitable and in a healthy position (unless we happen also to have another piece of data suggesting that the previous year's profits had been $5 million, in which case we may begin to wonder if something is going wrong). Seeing a traffic light change from green to red conveys the information that the cars around us are about to stop and that we should stop our car too.

信息

　　Knowledge　Knowledge is the accumulated store of information and data we carry around in our minds, together with our own interpretation of them based on reason, instinct and prior experience. If we read that the company's profits have declined from $5 million to $3.2 million, then we will know—thanks to our experience of such matters—that declining profits mean the company may be having troubles, and profits might decline still further next year. If we see a traffic light turn from green to red, our experience of driving tells us to stop and wait until the light turns green again before moving off. We would know these things: but a Kung bushman from the Kalahari desert, who has never seen a traffic light, and never read a compa-

知识

ny annual report, would not, simply because the data and the information would convey nothing to him. Knowledge is thus both contingent on data and information, and has an effect on our understanding of them.

知识管理

Knowledge management Knowledge management is a new subdiscipline of management which focuses on how to deliberately create and use knowledge more effectively, and aims to turn knowledge into value. It is usually seen as a 'general' management task, something which all managers do; it is not a separate function, like marketing or human resources, but a basic element to all management. Central to knowledge management is the knowledge transformation process, through which knowledge is acquired or created, stored and used.

信息技术

Information technology Modern theories of knowledge are heavily dependent on information technology (IT), sometimes also known as information and communications technology (ICT). Desktop, laptop and palm computers, linked through Internet or satellite relay systems, and loaded with various types of software for capturing, storing and using knowledge, are the main relevant forms, but more sophisticated technology up to and including artificial intelligence also has a role to play.

DISTINCTIONS 区别

In definitions, above, we made a distinction between three key concepts, *data*, *information* and *knowledge*. It is worth talking a little bit more about this, because the three terms are often confused. People often talk about 'taking another look at the data', when they might really mean looking again at the information the data are conveying to us. Information and knowledge are similarly often confused.

The distinction between these is admittedly a fine one. Max Boisot, a theorist of culture and communication who currently teaches in Barcelona, Spain, perhaps summed it up best when he said that data is a property of things, whereas knowledge is a property of people. Data have an existence independent of ourselves; they exist all around us. Information is the messages the data send us. Knowledge is the interpretation and understanding that we then give to that information.

Let us go back to our example of the company annual report. Annual reports tend to provide columns of data, summarizing the company's financial position and often giving current financial ratios of the kind we described in the previous chapter. Those data are simply numbers. If we have just arrived from the Kalahari desert and have never seen an annual report, we will not know what these numbers mean; we might not even recognize them as numbers! However, if we have some background knowledge (what numbers are, what the figures in the columns actually mean), we can see that the numbers are actually sending us signals: the company is doing well (or is not doing well), the company is working efficiently with low costs, and so on. These signals are what we call information.

But we still need to interpret that information. On their own, these signals do not necessarily mean much. The company is making a profit: what action is then called for on our part? Costs are low: do we need to do anything to make them still lower? But if we can put all these signals together and form a clear picture of what the company is doing, we can then *know* what the real position is. If we are aware of the company's past history and competitive environment, we can see that although profits are good, they could be better; costs are low, but they could be lower.

This leads us to an important conclusion: knowledge is needed in order to create knowledge. We need prior knowledge in order to interpret the signals and information that come to us. That is why in management today, so much stress is placed on learning, not only before managers start their careers but continuously throughout their careers. Learning is one way that managers acquire the knowledge that they need to make them function.

TYPES OF KNOWLEDGE 知识类型

Knowledge comes in different types and forms, but the most important division is between tacit knowledge and explicit knowledge. The distinction between these was first made by the sociologist Michael Polanyi in the 1950s, but has since been greatly amplified by theorists of knowledge management such as Nonaka Ikujiro and Max Boisot.

Explicit knowledge is knowledge that we can easily formulate, write down or put into speech and pass on to others. In the terminology of knowledge management, it can be easily codified. Explicit knowledge is often based heavily on easily provable factual data and on reason. Teaching someone how to drive an ordinary car or to play the piano or to write a marketing plan constitutes passing on explicit knowledge. Explicit knowledge is often widely available, or if not, can be easily communicated.

Tacit knowledge, on the other hand, is hard to formulate and express. Often it is very personal to ourselves; we *know* what we are doing, but we cannot express it to others in terms that make any sense. Tacit knowledge is often based on soft data and on intuition. Teaching someone to drive a Formula One racing car, or to conduct an orchestra, or to understand what the results of marketing research mean are all examples of passing on tacit knowledge.

Often tacit and explicit knowledge are present together. In this book, I have provided a considerable quantity of explicit knowledge. I have explained what strategy is, how organizations can be structured, the importance of marketing, the nature of production systems, the duties of a human resource management department. But what I have almost certainly not done is actually provided you with the knowledge of what it is actually like to *be* a manager. Even though I have both managed my own business and taught other managers for many years, I cannot simply lay out for you in writing on a printed page what it really feels like to practise management (possibly a great artist could do so; Leo Tolstoy, for example, conveyed very vividly what it was like to be on a battlefield in *War and Peace*, but I, alas, am not Tolstoy). That is tacit knowledge, and you will only be able to learn that by experiencing management for yourselves.

Which is more important, tacit knowledge or explicit knowledge? In Western organizations, we have tended to emphasize explicit knowledge, partly because it is easier to transmit but also for cultural reasons; since the seventeenth century, at least, our societies have tended to value 'scientific' (i. e. explicit) knowledge over that obtained through intuition. According to Nonaka, however, Eastern organizations tend to value tacit knowledge more highly, because it tends to be deeper and more creative, and also unique to the individual or organization that holds it. Nonaka gives the example of a famous Japanese baseball player, a man who broke records in Japan but who could not articulate why he was so successful. For Nonaka, unlocking this man's tacit knowledge would make his gifts available to other players.

This is quite true, and athletes and sporting figures and musicians who can pass on tacit knowledge tend to make excellent coaches and conductors. But explicit knowledge cannot simply be dismissed. As well as the tacit knowledge that makes a baseball star able to divine the pitcher's intentions and swing the bat at exactly the right moment to hit a home run, he (or she) also needs some more mundane explicit knowledge, such as familiarity with the rules of baseball, how to hold and grip a bat, where to stand over the plate and so on. Explicit knowledge may be less exciting, but it also tends to make up the background knowledge that we turn to when interpreting information and creating new knowledge for ourselves.

KNOWLEDGE MANAGEMENT
知识管理

Business and individuals process knowledge in much the same way that they process raw materials and parts to create products. The description of knowledge management that follows shows both how it works and why it is so important to management.

知识管理的目的是把知识转化为价值。

The purpose of knowledge management is to turn knowledge into value. It does this by *transforming* knowledge from 'raw' knowledge created or gleaned from the environment into something that is of use to the company or its customers. The kinds of uses to which knowledge can be put are nearly endless, and span the whole range of management activities: new products and services for customers, new and better ways of making things, better information about the market or about competitors, more skills and learning by employees; the list goes on.

This transforming of knowledge is a three-stage process. First, the business acquires knowledge, either by creating it internally or by learning from sources outside the organization. Second, it then catalogues and stores knowledge in ways that make it accessible when needed and easily transmitted. Finally, it puts knowledge to use in practical ways that create value.

KNOWLEDGE ACQUISITION
知识收集

Knowledge acquisition is simply the process of learning knowledge from other sources. We acquire knowledge by reading books, by taking training courses, by looking around and taking in information from the environment. Most of the knowledge we acquire in this way is explicit knowledge, though sometimes we find teachers or coaches or mentors who help us learn tacit knowledge as well. Much of this knowledge, as noted, is background knowledge, and it is said that the primary purpose of most education programmes is to teach people how to learn, to give them the techniques and background skills they need in order to contextualize information and absorb new knowledge.

It has been shown that organizations learn very much in the same way that individuals do, and just as an organization is greater than the sum of its parts, so the learning an organization gains is greater than the total learning of its individual members. Members of an organization who learn—especially if they learn together—will share experiences, impressions and items of knowledge, thus ensuring a broader learning experience and general outlook. Most businesses engage in knowledge acquisition, even if informally, on an ongoing basis; managers read the financial papers, staff go on training courses, etc. and people then swap experiences and knowledge circulates through the group. Nonaka Ikujiro found that this kind of informal learning was probably the best way to acquire both tacit and explicit knowledge.

KNOWLEDGE CREATION 知识创造

Not everything can be learned in the wider world, and organizations that wish to be competitive must ultimately begin to learn for themselves. Again, this can be done two ways: formally, through specially constituted research and development (R&D) departments or teams, and informally through the circulation of knowledge around the business as a whole.

R&D departments or teams consist of managers and other staff whose sole function is to generate new knowledge which may be of use to the company. Global businesses like IBM will employ many thousands of people engaged in R&D around the world. Some of these people will be engaged in theoretical or 'blue skies' work which has no direct relation to customer value, but is intended instead to push back the frontiers of knowledge more generally, creating opportunities that can be exploited later. Others will be looking at emerging technologies and their potential for exploitation; still others will be actively engaged in designing and building new products.

But although the R&D department may be the creative hub of the organization, other departments will engage in research as well. Marketing, as noted in Chapter 5, carries out research often on an ongoing basis into customer needs and consumer behaviour. Human resources carries out research on the views and motivations of staff. Financial managers may research new accounting methods or financial instruments, sometimes alone, sometimes in partnership with academic researchers in business schools. All this adds to the amount of knowledge the company creates.

And there is a second form of knowledge creation as well, through casual, informal conversations as people relate experiences, compare notes and bounce ideas off each other through e-mail discussions, during coffee breaks or over lunch. Many good ideas have been developed in many companies through just such informal exchanges, and many companies try to foster such discussions in hopes of generating new ideas. Companies such as Sony and Intel are famous for their discussion forums where people throw new ideas into the ring and let others discuss them and improve upon them.

It should be added that a great deal of the knowledge that a business and its people acquire may have no immediately apparent relevance to the business or its customers. One of the tasks of knowledge management is to determine what kinds of knowledge or which particular areas are most important, and try to focus attention on these as far as possible. However, it is equally important not to narrow the field of study or research too far. Many kinds of knowledge may prove to be relevant, but sometimes not until long after they have been acquired. This means that the storage of knowledge until it is needed becomes a second major issue for knowledge management.

KNOWLEDGE STORAGE　知识存储

Once created or acquired, knowledge then has to be stored. The main issues when considering knowledge storage are capacity, preservation and accessibility.

Prior to the invention of the computer, knowledge was stored on 'hard copy' records, ranging from the clay tablets and papyrus of the ancient world to hand-written or typewritten paper in our own times. Books, magazines, films, microfilms and so on stored knowledge that has been acquired or learned, while paper notes, file cards and the like stored knowledge generated within the firm. In large firms especially, physical capacity for storing records was limited, and in some cases companies had to destroy older records in order to make room for new ones. The computer has largely solved the capacity issue, with a single CD-ROM able to hold the same information as dozens of printed volumes.

Accessibility, however, remains an issue. In hard copy systems, anyone wishing to consult records had to know in which volume or box file to look. In computer systems, the same person must know which file to open. Critical to maintaining accessibility are tools such as database software, which allows the user to 'interrogate' the stored knowledge, asking a question and having the database indicate in which files the answers might be found. Even more sophisticated are management information systems (MIS) which collate tens of thousands or hundreds of thousands of points of knowledge and then present these in summary form, allowing the user to then 'drill down' and investigate in more detail those items of particular interest. These tools need to be carefully designed to ensure ease for the user, who often needs to find knowledge quickly without being distracted by clumsy operating systems.

Preservation also remains an important issue. Here again knowledge management comes up against the issue of which knowledge to keep and which to throw away on the grounds that it will not yield value. Sometimes the decision is obvious: a company making combine harvesters will not wish to acquire or keep knowledge about players in the National Basketball League. But to a company making running shoes, such information might be very valuable indeed; the company might want to approach players to promote its running shoes in an advertising campaign. Ultimately, common sense and fitness for purpose will dictate which knowledge should be preserved and which discarded; there are no hard and fast rules.

Closely related to knowledge storage is knowledge transmission, which allows knowledge, once stored, to freely circulate around the business. In general, it is considered that knowledge should circulate as freely as possible by allowing everyone in the business access to databases of knowledge. However, this may not always be desirable. Senior management may feel, for example, that it does not wish lower level employees to have knowledge of sensitive financial issues such as potential take-overs-or indeed, of the salaries being paid to the senior managers themselves. When and where barriers to access are employed depends on the company and its present situation, and it should be noted that there may be ethical and legal considerations here as well; by barring some employees from access to knowledge but granting it to others, is the company behaving ethically, and is it within the boundaries of local laws?

Finally, while computers and hard copy records are very important for knowledge storage, the most powerful storage device yet known remains the human brain. Although the mind is far from perfect, and can forget or lose knowledge in ways that computers cannot, only the mind can make the kinds of connections that create and store tacit knowledge. The brains of an organization's people contain its greatest and most valuable knowledge.

KNOWLEDGE USE　知识使用

Finally there comes the point when knowledge is put to use, in the form of new products, new processes or new ways of doing business more generally. To repeat, the ultimate aim of knowledge is to add value. Opinions still differ as to whether and how the value of knowledge can be measured, but increasingly the view is coming to be that an organization's collected knowledge should be measured and reported in financial statements as it represents an asset.

The problem with this view is that knowledge of itself is static, and is therefore a potential asset only. Not until knowledge is actually employed by people working on a new product or new process does that value actually become real. Further, we have seen that people use knowledge in a variety of small, incremental ways such as developing better understandings of markets, employee motivation and so on that, although ultimately contributing to value, is hard to define. Ultimately, the use of knowledge and its management is partly, at least, subjective and intuitive. It is for this reason that one of the greatest management thinkers, Peter Drucker, has described management as an art and not a science. Judgement and intuition as well as calculation are required, and nowhere is this more apparent than in the field of knowledge.

摘要

● 知识管理的目标是把知识转化为价值。

● 知识目前被当作公司最重要的资产。

● 知识的管理包括知识通过研究和学习的产生，知识的储存和传播，以及最终用于创造价值。

● 归根结底，知识的管理部分是直觉，基于一般常识和判断，而不是计算。

SUGGESTIONS FOR FURTHER READING
延伸阅读

Knowledge management is a growing field and new works are appearing all the time, but many are technical in nature and focus on technology systems for knowledge management. The following are more thoughtful and considered works on key issues.

Boisot, M. , *Information Space: A Framework for Learning in Organizations, Institutions and Culture*, London: Routledge, 1995.

Technical in places, but worth sticking with; the chapters on knowledge and communication are very important.

Cortada, J. W. (ed.) *The Rise of the Knowledge Worker*, Oxford: Butterworth-Heinemann, 1998.

A good look at the problems of managing people as knowledge workers.

De Geus, A. , *The Living Company: Habits for Survival in a Turbulent Environment*, London: Nicholas Brealey, 1997.

A very fine and readable book by one of the founding fathers of modern knowledge management.

Nonaka, I. and Takeuchi, H. , *The Knowledge-Creating Company*, Oxford: Oxford University Press, 1995.

Compares and contrasts the management of knowledge in Japanese and Western companies, with some valuable lessons for the latter.

Senge, P. M. , *The Fifth Discipline: The Art and Practice of the Learning Organisation*, New York: Doubleday, 1990.

A worldwide bestseller in the early 1990s, now a little dated, but still worth reading.

CULTURE

文　化

Culture is the collective programming of the mind which distinguishes the members of one human group from another.

（Geert Hofstede）

文化是区分不同社会或群体成员的一种心理聚合程序。

——吉尔特·霍夫斯塔德

Put very simply, culture means the values, customs, beliefs and behaviours held in common by a group of people. This group can be very large—we sometimes speak of 'Western culture' to mean the whole of Europe, North America, and Australia/New Zealand-or very small, as in the case of a golf club or a sporting team which has a particular ethos and way of doing things.

We have chosen somewhat unusually to give culture a separate chapter in this book simply because it affects so much of what managers do and how they think. Culture is usually considered in one of two forms: (1) the culture of organizations, usually considered as a sub-set of the field of organization behaviour, and (2) national and regional cultures, usually considered in the light of how they impact on marketing and human resource management. However, it is not common to discuss both these forms side by side. However, the two have similar effects on managers and how they think and work and make decisions. This short chapter will consider the two kinds of culture side by side and show how they impact on management, and on each other.

WHY IS CULTURE SO IMPORTANT?
为什么文化如此重要

In 2000, one of the largest and most significant mergers in corporate history took place when the Internet service provider AOL merged with the global media group Time Warner. The new combined company, AOL/Time Warner, was hailed as a 'new generation' company which would bring media and Internet communications together to create a new kind of global corporation. Sadly, as the newspapers would later report, things did not work out that way. Just a few years later, in 2002, AOL/Time Warner lost a staggering one hundred billion dollars, the largest annual loss in US corporate history.

What went wrong? There were many possibly explanations offered, but one contributing factor which seems to have been almost universally agreed by those outside the organization was that the two companies that merged had fundamentally different cultures. AOL, a new company, was very much a 'new style' company whose managers adopted an aggressive approach to competitors and even to each other and worked in a high-pressure atmosphere. Time Warner, an older company, had a more laid-back approach, and its managers tended to value harmony and conciliation rather than aggression and confrontation. None of these things could be quantified or stated as proven facts, but to observers of both organizations they were well-known phenomena. Quite simply, the two groups of managers could not understand each other, did not like each other, and could not work with each other. And while other and more serious problems and errors occurred, the gap in understanding between the two cultures proved to be a hole which could swallow up a hundred billion dollars.

Other examples can be found in plenty. Recall the case of the accounting and consultancy firm Arthur Andersen, discussed in Chapter 3, where two different and rival cultures emerged within the same organization and then engaged in a struggle for power. When cultures clash, even the largest and most powerful organizations become unstable and can be brought to the point of collapse.

Nor does there necessarily have to be a clash of cultures; a single culture can itself, through its views and attitudes, bring a business down. In Britain, in the 1950s, not just one but many businesses failed because of an entrenched institutional culture among British managers that refused to recognize the need for change. Training and education, which could have solved many problems, were persistently hampered by lack of support from managers at the senior levels. When the Federation of British Industries, the main industrial association in Britain, passed a resolution at an annual general meeting stating that ' managers were made rather than born ' and that managerial competence was a result of training and education rather than inborn talent, the head of the organization, Sir Charles Renold, resigned in protest. This culture of stagnation led to British industry failing to modernize and to thousands of companies losing their markets to more aggressive and modern competitors from the USA, Germany and Japan. Many of these companies were either sold or went bankrupt.

But culture is not just a negative influence. On the positive side, a progressive culture that works well can be a huge source of inspiration and creativity. There is no one single recipe for this kind of culture: the pressure-cooker atmosphere of Microsoft and the more relaxed and laid-back cultures of Sony and Intel serve equally well as seed-beds for creative thinking. In each case, management has sought to build a culture that will stimulate creativity, and in each case it has succeeded. And the fusion of cultures, though difficult to achieve, can also bring about more inspiration and creativity. The merger of European car-maker Renault with its former rival the Japanese company Nissan has been praised for bringing the best of European and Japanese thinking together, and will probably ensure that Renault-Nissan survives in the increasingly competitive global car market.

ORGANIZATION CULTURE　组织文化

The comments above relate to organization cultures, and we will come on to the impact of national culture in a moment. Let us begin by briefly dissecting the concept of corporate culture and examining just what it is. At the start of this chapter we defined culture as the values, customs, beliefs and behaviours held in common by a group of people, in this case a business organization. One can understand more about the culture of any particular organization by asking some of the following questions:

价值观

- *Values*—what sorts of values do members of the organization have in common? Do they value hard work, teamwork, training? Do they value their own leisure time, fun and games, the cameraderie of office life? Do they value respect for superiors, or personal freedom and independence at work? Do they feel that work comes first, or do they treat work as a necessary evil?

习俗

- *Customs*—does the organization have any special customs, such as dress-down Friday or a tradition of get-togethers outside of office hours? Do members of the organization have any special connection with each other, or do they keep largely to themselves? Do they have common interests, or are they a group of largely disparate individuals?

- *Beliefs*—do members of the organization believe in the organization itself? Do they agree with its aims and goals. Do people at lower levels sympathize, at least to some extent, with senior managers? Do people think the organization is fundamentally a good place to work?

  信仰

- *Behaviours*—what common behaviours do people show? Do they tend to arrive promptly for work, or do they have a lackadaisical attitude to time-keeping? Are they respectful or contemptuous of authority? Do they keep their workstations tidy, or are the latter usually a mess? Do they take up training and other development opportunities when offered, or do they prefer to keep their distance? Are they polite and friendly to customers, or rude and dismissive?

  行为

The answers to these questions are indicators only; culture cannot be quantified. We mentioned in Chapter 2 that some consultants say they can actually 'feel' or 'smell' the culture of a business through various cues and stimuli in the environment; whether premises are kept clean, whether people are friendly or unfriendly to strangers and so on. The anthropologist Clifford Geertz in his study of cultures suggested that cultures could also be classified according to 'thickness' or 'thinness': a 'thick' culture is one where the values, beliefs and so on are widespread and deeply held and will be difficult to change, while a 'thin' culture is not strongly held and easier to change.

By answering the questions above and looking at the issue of thickness and thinness, we can form some overall views of what a particular culture might be like. Here are some examples of corporate culture (note that these are not mutually exclusive, and actual cultures might partake of more than one of the following):

文化的类型

- *Conservative*: the culture adheres to present values and tends to resist change.

  保守型

- *Progressive*: the culture is forward-looking and amenable to change.

  进步型

激进型

- *Aggressive*: the culture takes a proactive approach to competition and innovation and believes the organization should dominate its market.

和谐型

- *Harmonious*: the culture favours co-existence between groups within the organization and between organizations, and tends to recognize and accept diversity.

被动型

- *Passive*: the culture is less competitive and tends to be content with the status quo.

创新型

- *Innovative*: the culture believes in innovation as a force for improving the organization, society, or both, and will actively promote innovation without direction from above.

创业型

- *Entrepreneurial*: the culture is individualistic and democratic and rewards personal enterprise.

家长型

- *Patriarchal*: the culture looks to its leaders for guidance and tends not to reward personal enterprise.

技术导向型

- *Technology-oriented*: the culture believes in the power of technology as an article of faith, and eagerly adopts new technology.

人文型

- *Humanistic*: the culture is strongly centred on human values and human relationships, seeing these as the heart of the business. It may be sceptical of the value of technology.

Other features may be noticeable as well. To sum up, every organization has a culture, and that culture in turn determines the organization's attitude to a great many things: its customers, its products, its goals and values, its suppliers and its own members. It affects the relationships between people, and can determine whether communications work effectively and knowledge is circulated. In the end, it can influence the success or failure of management.

In Chapter 2, we discussed the kinds of changes that organization cultures can undergo, and some of the ways that change may be planned and carried out. To briefly recapitulate, changing the culture of an organization is very hard, and requires patience, determination and leadership. Changing the culture of an organization is often a pre-requisite to changing the organization itself, especially where a conservative or passive culture has been allowed to develop. Again, Geertz's concept of thickness and thinness comes into play, with 'thick' cultures being harder to change and uproot.

Finally, it should be recognized that different parts of the organization might develop sub-cultures all their own. Marketing departments, for example, often have a built-in bias towards more humanistic cultures, while production departments might become more technology-oriented. As we saw with Arthur Andersen and AOL/Time Warner, some parts of an organization might have a more aggressive approach to competition while others will value harmony. There is nothing intrinsically wrong with having these different sub-cultures, and it may prove difficult to eradicate them. The potential for harm lies when different sub-cultures adopt different and opposing values, customs, beliefs and behaviours, and then find that they cannot live with each other within the framework of the organization. The resulting conflict can paralyze or even kill the business.

NATIONAL CULTURES 民族文化

National cultures are again shared sets of values, customs, beliefs and behaviours that are held in common by most or all of the citizens of a country or a significant ethnic grouping (we are using the word national here in a loose sense; it is recognized that many nations such as Spain, India, Malaysia and so on have several different 'national' cultures). While an organization's culture is a feature of the organization itself, national culture is part of the environment. Its consequences for business are several:

- It shapes the values and beliefs of customers, meaning that customer behaviour and decision-making may vary from culture to culture.

- It affects social perceptions of business—and in particular foreign businesses—and can have an impact on the legal and regulatory frameworks that govern business conduct.
- It affects the motivations of employees and how they behave in the workplace, particularly with regard to hierarchy and responsibility.
- Following from the above, national culture also has a determining effect on organization culture and helps to shape the latter; thus conservative national cultures are more likely to produce conservative organizational cultures, patriarchal national cultures are more likely to produce patriarchal organizational cultures, and so on.

The impact of national culture on customer behaviour and decision-making was touched on in Chapter 5, when we looked at marketing across different cultures. Often simple things such as names, words, colours and so on can have a dramatic impact on customer perceptions, either positive or negative. Coca-Cola is one company which has persistently been able to use images and words to its advantage, adapting itself to different cultures around the world. One of its few mistakes was in Taiwan, when an early and poor translation of the slogan 'Coke adds life' was interpreted to literally mean 'Coke will bring back your ancestors from the grave.' But this error was quickly fixed, and when entering mainland China Coca-Cola chose for its logo a set of characters that were pronounced *ke kou ke le*; the literal meaning in Mandarin is 'mouth thirsty getting joy'. This not only reinforced the Coca-Cola name but gave it a resonance in the local culture. Although globalization (see below) is slowly breaking down some of the barriers between national markets, many still remain.

Social perceptions of business can range from the dramatically different, such as the prohibition on charging interest on bank loans in Islamic cultures, to more subtle shifts such as the 'corporatist' culture found in some European states, notably Italy. Here, businesses and government work closely together in a way that would be considered unthinkable—even unethical—in the United States. These different social expectations of what business is and how managers should behave are often expressed in the laws and business regulations of different countries.

The final two points, concerning employee behaviour and motivation and the impact that national culture has on local culture, were studied in detail by the Dutch academic Geert Hofstede in the 1970s and 1980s. Although it was known anecdotally that different national cultures had different perceptions of work, motivation and hierarchy, Hofstede set out to prove that such differences existed. By conducting global surveys of managers and employees of IBM (for which he had worked for many years), Hofstede was not only able to show that these differences existed, but also to come up with a scheme for categorizing them. According to Hofstede, cultural differences could be measured by scoring employee attitudes on four dimensions: power distance, uncertainty avoidance, individualism/collectivism and masculinity/femininity. Power distance measures how power is distributed within a society; high power distance societies have strong hierarchies, while low power distance societies have weak and loose hierarchies. In uncertainty avoidance, societies with high scores are intolerant of risk and change, while low scores show that risk and paradox are more widely accepted. On the individualism/collectivism scale, high scores reflect the importance of personal freedom and free will, while low scores require a degree of subjugation of the individual will to the needs of the community. Finally, in masculinity/femininity, societies where earnings, promotion and status are seen as the most important work goals are classified as 'masculine', while those where quality of life and human relationships are prioritized are classified as 'feminine'.

Using these four dimensions, Hofstede classified more than sixty national cultures in terms of their approach to work. America and Scandinavian countries scored low on power distance, while China and Japan scored more highly. Indonesia and Malaysia scored highly on uncertainty avoidance, while some European countries had very low scores, and so on. Using these four dimensions, Hofstede was able to build up a series of composite pictures of national culture and how it impacts on the workplace.

Hofstede's conclusions and methods have been challenged, but interestingly, almost no one has questioned his conclusion that cultural variations make a huge difference in how different cultures perceive work, hierarchy, motivation and the like. On the contrary, most critics have insisted that Hofstede did not go far enough in measuring these differences, and that even more complex dimensions and differences exist. Few would challenge the basic assumption that different national cultures shape and affect attitudes to work around the world.

WORKING ACROSS CULTURES
跨文化经营

The problems of working in different cultures become still stronger when companies work *across* cultures, as for example when a multinational company sells products made in one country in a different national market, or when managers who have been educated and have worked in one culture are sent to work in another culture. The problems currently faced by American and European managers sent to work in subsidiaries in China exemplify this. Managers from the former are used to more or less democratic workplaces in which workers take a certain amount of personal responsibility and will be intolerant of overly directive leaders. In China, however, thanks in part to the conditioning of years of authoritarian rule under the Maoist system, workers expect leaders to give directions and make decisions, and are often unhappy at taking personal responsibility. This clash of cultures often leads to misunderstandings and sometimes to severe problems when American managers simply assume a task will be carried out without their having to give orders.

Western managers working in Asia—and vice versa—will often have other and more personal problems. Expatriate managers, as they are known, have to live as well as work in these different cultures, and this can mean further problems for families who must either accompany their husband/wife or be separated from them for long periods of time. The managing of these expatriates poses special challenges for the human resources function.

GLOBALIZATION AND DIVERSITY
全球化与多样性

Over the past three decades, thanks again in part to better information technology, the world of business has been steadily shrinking. It is now comparatively easy to manage a business with operations and customers in many different parts of the world. Communications which formerly took days or weeks can now be handled in a matter of a few minutes. It is sometimes argued that this in turn is leading to what is known as convergence, with global markets and cultures becoming more and more similar. The success of global brands like McDonald's, Coca-Cola and Nike is cited as an example of this. Eventually, it is argued, markets and cultures everywhere will look more or less the same.

The counter-argument accepts that there is a degree of convergence going on, but questions how quickly this is happening and how far it will go. (There is another set of arguments over whether convergence is a good thing, but these are not strictly speaking relevant to the basics of management.) Some observers believe that things such as global common interests in music, television and fashion have been overstated, and that the emergence of 'new' cultural forms like bhangra music and Hong Kong cinema mean that even though cultural forms can be spread globally, there will always be a plurality of cultures; Hollywood will increasingly have to compete with 'Bollywood', the powerful and productive Indian film industry, on a global basis. In other words, globalization is happening, but it is not simply the dominance of Western culture that might have been predicted. Others believe that there will be a backlash, that local cultures will experience a resurgence, and point to issues such as increasing nationalist sentiment in many parts of the world as evidence of this.

For today's manager, globalization is a reality that must be faced, but so too is the evidence of continuing global diversity. For the foreseeable future, culture will continue to be an issue affecting many aspects of management.

摘要

- 文化是企业中一个非常重要的因素，包括组织文化和民族文化都有影响力。

- 文化不能量化，但是对所有的思考和决策过程都有作用。

- 在同一个组织里可以存在两种或更多的文化，这种多样性可能是一种积极的力量，但是避免价值观的冲突很重要。

- 民族文化对组织文化和整个的市场和社会都有影响。

- 全球化可能正在减少文化的力量，但文化仍然在发挥强大的影响力。

SUGGESTIONS FOR FURTHER READING
延伸阅读

Adler, .N. J., *International Dimensions of Organizational*

Behavior, 4th edn, Cincinnati, OH: South-Western College Publishing.

Very useful textbook on the influence of culture on people and organizations, in particular the opening chapter.

Hampden-Turner, C. and Trompenaars, F. , *The Seven Cultures of Capitalism*, Garden City, NY: Doubleday, 1993.

Very readable and enjoyable, and thought-provoking on the subject of how different cultures approach business.

Hofstede, G. , *Cultures and Organizations: Software of the Mind*, London: McGraw-Hill, 1991.

The second of Hofstede's two highly influential books, and the most up to date. Many people have criticized Hofstede, but almost no one has said his ideas are not valid; most complain that he does not go far enough!

Ohmae, K. , *The Borderless World: Power and Strategy in the Interlinked Economy*, New York: Harper Business, 1990.

One of the classic texts on globalization; read and see whether you agree with the author.

THE MANAGER

管 理 者

We have not put our trust in kings; let us not put it in natural resources, but grasp the truth that exhaustless wealth lies in the latent and as yet undeveloped capacities of individuals, of corporations, of states. Instead of oppression from the top, engendering antagonisms and strife, ambitious pressure should come from the bottom, guidance and assistance from the top.

(Harrington Emerson)

我们还没有把我们的信任放在领导者身上；让我们不要把它放在自然资源上，而是抓住一个事实：用之不竭的财富存在于个人、企业、国家潜在以及尚未开发的能力中。压力不是来自于产生对立和冲突的上层，艰巨的压力应该来自底层，而指导和协助才应该来自于上层。

——哈林顿·爱默生

Let us close this examination of the basics of management by looking very briefly at one of the most important basics: the manager himself or herself. 'The manager' is not often a subject of study in management training and education programmes, but this chapter will hopefully help the reader to: (1) tie up a few loose ends from earlier chapters, and (2) develop a more personal approach to their studies and work. The following are issues that will impact on a manager at some point, and, just as with the other more formal disciplines of management, the time to begin considering these is during the earliest stages of training and development.

MANAGERIAL CAREERS
管理作为一种职业

First, as Chapter 3 suggested, managerial careers do not follow a smooth path. A few generations ago, a manager—indeed, any worker—might expect to join a business as a young person and, provided the business remained sound and the manager himself or herself was competent, remain with that business until retirement forty or so years later. This does still happen, but it is becoming increasingly rare. Businesses are constantly reshaping and changing themselves, and business activities that were considered essential one year may be redundant by the following year. Most managers can expect to have their jobs disappear out from under them at least once in their career; many managers spend a fair portion of their time anticipating when this will happen and focusing on how to move on before it actually does happen.

At the same time, the constant shaping and reshaping of companies mean that many new jobs will open up. Writers on management career structures increasingly talk of 'portfolio careers', with managers changing jobs and companies every few years in pursuit of new opportunities. These opportunities are particularly available to highly skilled and qualified managers; those whose training is out of date or irrelevant to modern needs will have a much harder time finding new work. One of the mantras of modern management is 'lifelong learning' or 'careerlong learning'; managers must seek to constantly update their skills and knowledge if they are to be able to get well-paid and responsible jobs. In other words, the initial graduate or undergraduate training at the start of a career is just a first step; the manager needs to go on learning until the day he or she retires.

Increasingly, too, responsibility for this learning is becoming that of individual managers and not of the companies that employ them. While companies run training programmes, these are devoted to developing skills and knowledge that suit that company's needs. The manager has to be careful to ensure that personal needs for knowledge and skills are not neglected. In sum, the manager has to be prepared to take charge of his or her career, serving each employer faithfully and to the best of his or her ability, but always taking care that his or her own interests do not become entirely sublimated.

MANAGERIAL RESPONSIBILITIES
管理职责

The manager has a responsibility to himself or herself, but there are also other responsibilities. Businesses, especially very large businesses, are powerful entities, and they can have a great deal of impact on those around them. Every manager has responsibilities when it comes to dealing with colleagues, employees, customers, suppliers, government and society at large.

Managers must of course obey the law, even when laws may seem absurd. Taxes may be deemed unfair; they still have to be paid, and measures taken to reduce tax must be within the bounds of the law. But the law should not be the only guide to managerial conduct. All managers are also citizens, and they are guided by the same ethical rules that guide everyone else. One does not shed citizenship at the door of the office. Indeed, the power that many managers wield means that, if anything, their ethical responsibilities are even greater.

ETHICS 道德规范

Managing ethically is not easy. Conflicts will often arise.

Suppose a supplier in a foreign country asks managers to pay them an illegal bribe. If managers refuse, as they are perfectly entitled to do, this could mean the loss of business in the home country; a factory might have to be shut down, people would be put out of work. Which is the ethical choice? (The dilemma above might sound farfetched, but in fact Western companies dealing in countries with lax or badly enforced laws faced this problem frequently.)

Companies and industry associations try to help by drawing up codes of conduct which show managers what is expected of them in certain situations. But no code of conduct can cover every situation. Ultimately, the manager's own ethical beliefs must help them to decide what is right. It is therefore important that every manager has a clear understanding of what ethics are and how they guide behaviour towards others.

CORPORATE GOVERNANCE
公司治理

We discussed corporate governance in Chapter 7. Little needs to be added here save a reminder that managers, unless they own large numbers of shares themselves, do not own the companies they run. They are stewards, legally and morally responsible to the owners of the company, the shareholders. Amongthe principal responsibilities of the manager is a duty of care towards the shareholders. Actions which are against the interests of the shareholders are wrong, as is concealing information from shareholders for personal gain, or even out of fear that shareholders will not approve. This again poses some real dilemmas and conflicts of interest for managers, and each of these will have its own particular solution, to be worked out using a combination of knowledge of where responsibilities lie and common sense. But in no case should the manager put his or her personal interests ahead of those of the shareholders.

EXERCISING LEADERSHIP
领导力的行使

We noted in Chapter 1 that leadership and management are not entirely the same thing. John Kotter, probably the foremost American writer on leadership, has argued that while management focuses on co-ordination and execution, leadership focuses on planning and vision. Management is about the here-and-now; leadership is about the future. But Kotter does not believe that managers and leaders should be entirely separate people (although in many cases this does happen), but rather that management and leadership should be combined in the same person.

Managers should exercise leadership, even if only for the people around them. Leadership does not necessarily mean control over people; a leader is not required to have 'followers'. Rather, a leader in business terms is someone who generates new ideas, has the vision to see how those ideas can be developed and put into effect, and inspires those around him or her, through persuasion and example, to share that same vision. That, in essence, is what leadership in business requires. In the old days of strong hierarchies it was thought that this quality of leadership was only really necessary among managers at the very top of the organization. Today, we see that leadership is necessary everywhere, and that the organizations that are really successful are the ones where managers at all levels are willing to take charge, have an idea and see it through. Leadership is no longer restricted to the boardroom. Any manager can be a leader; and the managers that succeed are likely to be those with the greatest capacity for leadership.

CHALLENGES AND CRISES
挑战和危机

'The only constant factor in business is change' is a mantra often heard, especially in the 1990s. Some writers still adhere to this view, while others such as Jim Collins in *Good to Great* urge caution; some things are changing, others are not. But even if change itself is a variable thing, affecting some areas of business and some management tasks more than others, its presence still has to be recognized. Change is a constant. New technology appears, fashions and customer preferences change, competitors make sudden and unexpected moves, shareholders begin buying or selling shares for no apparent reason, governments introduce new laws, employee motivation changes as staff grow older and more experienced. All these things mean that the world of business is a constantly shifting kaleidoscope of small moving parts constantly resorting themselves.

Those who study managers at work, like Henry Mintzberg, note that managers seem to spend a high proportion of their time 'firefighting', dealing with sudden unplanned changes that emerge and require action. Often these changes are quite small, and a simple solution can be easily found. Sometimes they are more complex; occasionally they are massive, like the strategic inflection points described by Andrew Grove. The only way to deal with these is to ensure that the business is strong, healthy and flexible enough to deal with challenges and crises when they occur. That they will occur must be taken for granted; managers can control many things, but they cannot control everything in their environment. Any plan or forecast must take into account the possibility that the situation envisaged will not come to pass. A German military strategist, Field-Marshal von Moltke, once remarked that 'No plan survives contact with the enemy.' In fact, the simple statement 'No plan survives' would have been equally accurate.

Paradoxically, as Jim Collins argues, managing through times of change actually requires even more attention to the basics of management. Just as important as knowing what to change is knowing what not to change. Powerful though the forces of change are, some eternal verities remain. Every business needs a goal; to reach that goal it requires an organization; to make that organization work it needs people. Businesses need customers; customers need products and services; knowledge of what customers need and how to make it will allow the business to supply customers and make a profit; capital investment is needed before production begins. Keeping these truths in mind allows the study of management to become simpler, and can help give structure and pattern to the mass of knowledge and information the student will receive. And ultimately, it will make the tasks of management simpler as well.

摘要

● 管理职业并不是平坦的路，在职业生涯中，一个管理者有望多次改变工作、职责和老板。

● 如同管理自己职业的变化一样，管理者也需要擅长应对环境和组织中的变化。

● 尽管管理和领导不同，所有的管理人员需要表现出领导力，尤其是在像对于企业所有者负有的道德责任和行为方面。

SUGGESTIONS FOR FURTHER READING
延伸阅读

Bennis, W. G. and Nanus, B., *Leaders*, Reading, MA: Addison-Wesley, 1985.

One of the classic studies of leadership, including the many problems that leaders must face. Very readable and informative.

Cadbury, A., *The Company Chairman*, Hemel Hempstead: Director Books, 2nd edn, 1995.

Written for a British audience, this was a bestseller in America as well, and talks about the moral and ethical dimensions to management and leadership.

Follett, M. P. , *Creative Experience*, New York: Longmans Green, 1924.

The bestselling management book of the 1920s, this isn't about management at all, but is about power, control, co-ordination, responsibility, creativity and change. Each new generation of managers rediscovers this book all over again; be the first in your generation to do so!

Kotter, J. P. , *The General Managers*, New York: The Free Press, 1982.

A very fine study of management at the top level. See also his A Force for Change: How Leadership Differs from Management (*New York: The Free Press*, 1990).

Mintzberg, H. , *Mintzberg on Management*, New York: Free Press, 1989.

A collection of interesting and thought-provoking articles and essays by the Canadian guru.

参考文献

Adler, N. J. (2000) *International Dimensions of Organizational Behavior*, 4th edn, Cincinnati, OH: South-Western College Publishing.

Albert, S. and Bradley, K. (1997) *Managing Knowledge: Experts, Agencies and Organizations*, Cambridge: Cambridge University Press.

Ansoff, H. I. (1965) *Corporate Strategy*, New York: John Wiley and Sons.

Argyris, C. (1971) *Management and Organizational Development*, New York: McGraw-Hill.

Argyris, C. and Schön, D. (1978) *Organizational Learning*, Reading, MA: Addison-Wesley.

Babbage, C. (1835) *The Economy of Machinery and Manufactures*, London: Charles Knight.

Barbash, J. (1985) *The Elements of Industrial Relations*, Madison, WI: University of Wisconsin Press.

Barnard, C. A. (1983) *The Functions of the Executive*, Cambridge, MA: Harvard University Press.

Bennis, W. (1989) *On Becoming a Leader*, Reading, MA: Addison-Wesley.

—— (1993) *An Invented Life: Reflections on Leadership and Change*, Reading, MA: Addison-Wesley.

Bennis, W. G. and Nanus, B. (1985) *Leaders*, Reading, MA: Addison-Wesley.

Berle, A. A. and Means, G. C. (1932) *The Modern Corporation and Private Property*, New York: Macmillan.

Boisot, M. (1995) *Information Space: A Framework for Learning in Organizations, Institutions and Culture*, London: Routledge.

—— (1998) *Knowledge Assets: Securing Competitive Advantage in the Information Economy*, Oxford: Oxford University Press.

Burnham, J. (1941) *The Managerial Revolution: Or, What is Happening in the World Now*, New York: Putnam.

Burns, T. and Stalker, G. M. (1961) *The Management of Innovation*, London: Tavistock Publications.

Cadbury, E. (1912) *Experiments in Industrial Organization*, London: Longmans, Green & Co.

Chandler, A. D. (1962) *Strategy and Structure: Chapters in the History of American Industrial Enterprise*, Cambridge, MA: MIT Press.

—— (1977) *The Visible Hand: The Managerial Revolution in American Business*, Cambridge, MA: Harvard University Press.

Christensen, C. M. (1997) *The Innovator's Dilemma*, New York: HarperCollins.

Collins, J. (2001) *Good to Great*, New York: Random House, 2001.

Collins, J. and Porras, J. (1994) *Built to Last: Successful Habits of Visionary Companies*, New York: HarperBusiness.

Cortada, J. W. (ed.) (1998) *The Rise of the Knowledge Worker*, Oxford: Butterworth-Heinemann.

Crainer, S. and Clutterbuck, D. (1990) *Makers of Management*, London: Macmillan.

Crosby, P. B. (1979) *Quality is Free: The Art of Making Quality Certain*, New York: McGraw-Hill.

Cutcher-Gershenfeld, J. (1998) *Knowledge Driven Work*, Oxford: Oxford University Press.

Cyert, R. M. and March, J. G. (1963) *A Behavioural Theory of the Firm*, New York: Prentice Hall.

De Geus, A. (1997) *The Living Company: Habits for Survival in a Turbulent Environment*, London: Nicholas Brealey.

Deming, W. E. (1986) *Out of the Crisis*, Cambridge, MA: MIT Center for Advanced Engineering Study.

Drucker, P. (1954) *The Practice of Management*, London: Heron Books.

—— (1966) *The Effective Executive*, New York: Harper & Row.

—— (1974) *Management: Tasks, Responsibilities, Practices*, New York: Harper & Row.

—— (1989) *The New Realities*, Oxford: Heinemann.

Emerson, H. (1909) *Efficiency as a Basis for Operations and Wages*, New York: Engineering Magazine.

Fayol, H. (1984) *General and Industrial Management*, trans. I. Gray, New York: David S. Lake.

Follett, M. P. (1924) *Creative Experience*, New York: Longmans Green.

Ford, H. (1931) *Moving Forward*, New York: Garden City.

Gabor, A. (1990) *The Man Who Discovered Quality*, New York: Times Books.

Ghoshal, S. and Bartlett, C. A. (1997) *The Individualized Corporation*, New York: Harper Collins.

Grove, A. (1983) *High Output Management*, New York: Random House.

—— (1996) *Only the Paranoid Survive: How to Exploit the Crisis Points that Challenge Every Company and Career*, New York: Harper Collins.

Gulick, L. H. and Urwick, L. F. (eds) (1937) *Papers on the Science of Administration*, New York: Institute of Public Administration.

Hamel, G. and Prahalad, C. K. (1989) *Competing for the Future*, Boston: Harvard Business School Press.

Hampden-Turner, C. and Trompenaars, F. (1993) *The Seven Cultures of Capitalism*, Garden City, NY: Doubleday.

Handy, C. (1976) *Understanding Organisations*, London: Penguin.

—— (1989) *The Age of Unreason*, London: Business Books.

—— (1994) *The Empty Raincoat*, London: Hutchinson.

Hersberg, F. (1966) *Work and the Nature of Man*, Cleveland, OH: The World Publishing Company.

Hofstede, G. (1984) 'National Cultures Revisited', *Asia Pacific Journal of Management* 1: 22 –8.

—— (1991) *Cultures and Organisations: Software of the Mind*, London: McGraw-Hill.

Jay, A. (1967) *Management and Machiavelli*, London: Hodder & Stoughton.

Juran, J. (1989) *Juran on Leadership for Quality: An Executive Handbook*, New York: The Free Press.

Kanter, R. M. (1983) *The Change Masters: Innovation for Productivity in the American Corporation*, New York: Simon and Schuster.

Kaplan, R. S. and Norton, D. P. (1996) *The Balanced Scorecard: Translating Strategy into Action*, Boston: Harvard Business School Press.

Kotler, P. (1997) *Marketing Management*, Englewood Cliffs, NJ: Prentice-Hall.

Kotter, J. P. (1982) *The General Managers*, New York: The Free Press.

—— (1990) *A Force for Change: How Leadership Differs from Management*, New York:

The Free Press.

Lawrence, P. R. and Lorsch, J. (1969) *Developing Organizations: Diagnosis and Action*, Reading, MA: Addison-Wesley.

Levitt, T. (1983) *The Marketing Imagination*, New York: The Free Press.

March, J. G. and Simon, H. A. (1958) *Organizations*, Oxford: Blackwell.

Matsuhita, K. (1988) *Quest for Prosperity: The Life of a Japanese Industrialist*, Tokyo: PHP Institute.

McLuhan, M. (1964) *Understanding Media: The Extensions of Man*, London: Routledge & Kegan Paul.

Miles, R. E. and Snow, C. C. (1978) *Organizational Strategy, Structure and Process*, New York: McGraw-Hill.

Mintzberg, H. (1973) *The Nature of Managerial Work*, New York, Harper & Row.

—— (1989) *Mintzberg on Management*, New York: Free Press.

Mooney, J. D. and Reilley, A. C. (1931) *Onward Industry! The Principles of Organization and Their Significance to Modern Industry*, New York: Harper & Bros.

Morgan, G. (1986) *Images of Organization*, Newbury Park, CA: Sage.

Nonaka, I. and Takeuchi, H. (1995) *The Knowledge-Creating Company*, Oxford: Oxford University Press.

Ohmae, K. (1990) *The Borderless World: Power and Strategy in the Interlinked Economy*, New York: Harper Business.

Peters, T. and Waterman, R. H. (1982) *In Search of Excellence: Lessons from America's Best-Run Companies*, New York: Harper and Row.

Porter, M. (1980) *Competitive Strategy: Techniques for Analyzing Industries and Competitors*, New York: The Free Press.

—— (1985) *Competitive Advantage: Creating and Sustaining Superior Performance*, New York: The Free Press.

Roethlisberger, F. J. and Dickson, W. J. (1939) *Management and the Worker*, Cambridge, MA: Harvard University Press.

Schön, D. (1983) *The Reflective Practitioner*, New York: Basic Books.

Scott, W. D. (1913) *The Psychology of Advertising*, Chicago: Dodd, Mead.

Semler, R. (1993) *Maverick! The Success Story Behind the World's Most Unusual Workplace*, London: Arrow.

Senge, P. M. (1990) *The Fifth Discipline: The Art and Practice of the Learning Organisation*, New York: Doubleday.

Simon, H. , March, J. G. and Guetzkow, H. (1958) *Organizations*, New York: Wiley.

Snow, C. C. (ed.) (1989) *Strategy, Organization Design and Human Resource Management*, New York: JAI Press.

Squires, S. , Smith C. , Yeack, W. and McDougall, L. (2003) *Inside Arthur Andersen: Shifting Values, Unexpected Consequences*, London: FT Prentice Hall.

Taylor, F. W. (1911) *The Principles of Scientific Management*, New York: Harper and Row; repr. Norwalk CT: The Easton Press, 1993, with foreword by D. B. Sicilia.

Teece, D. J. (1987) *The Competitive Challenge*, New York: Harper & Row.

Warner, M. (ed.) (1998) *IEBM Handbook of Management Thinking*, London: International Thomson Business Press.

Whitehead, T. N. (1936) *Leadership in a Free Society: A Study in Human Relations Based on an Analysis of Present-Day Industrial Civilization*, London: Oxford University Press.

Witzel, M. (ed.) (2001) *Biographical Dictionary of Management*, Bristol: Thoemmes Press, 2 vols.

—— (2001) *Builders and Dreamers: The Making and Meaning of Management*, London: FT-Prentice Hall.

Womack, J. P. , Jones, D. T. and Roos, D. (1990) *The Machine that Changed the World*, New York: Macmillan.

Wren, D. and Greenwood, R. G. (1998) *Management Innovators: The People and Ideas That Have Shaped Modern Business*, New York: Oxford University Press.

Zeleny, M. (2000) 'Knowledge vs. Information', in M. Zeleny (ed.), *The IEBM Handbook of Information Technology in Business*, London: Thomson Learning.

主题词索引

持续改善 continuous improvement

合同 contracts

核心竞争力 core competency

公司财务 corporate finance

企业管理 corporate governance

成本关注 cost focus

成本领先 cost leadership

费用 costs

分化差异 cultural difference

文化多样性 cultural diversity

文化 culture

履历 curriculum vitae（CV）

客户满意度 customer delight

客户参与 customer involvement

客户保持 customer retention

客户 customer

数据 data

资产负债率 debt ratio

权力下放 decentralization

决策 decision-making

民主 democracy

民主化 democratization

部门 department

欲望 desire

分化 differentiation

直销 direct selling

歧视 discrimination

剥离 divest

网络公司 dotcoms

东印度公司 East India Company

成效 effectiveness

效率 efficiency

电子时代 electronic age

员工参与 employee involvement

员工 employee

就业法 employment law

创业 entrepreneurship

环境 environment

电子销售点 EPOS（electronic point of sale）

股权价值 equity value

道德行为 ethical behaviour

道德 ethics

评价 evaluation

执行董事 executive director

家庭 family

英国工业联合会 Federation of British Industry

财务会计 financial accounting

财务报表 financial statement

财务透明度 financial transparency

灵活性 flexibility

流量 flow

预测 forecasting

外币交易 foreign currency transactions

一线单位 front-line units

函数 function

期货市场 futures market

资产负债 gearing

全球流动 global flow

全球生产 global production

全球化 globalization

目标 goal

团队 group

增长 growth

增长预测 growth forecast

收获 harvest

猎头公司 head hunters

有机组织 organic organization

组织 organization

组织文化 organization culture

组织理论 organization theory

组织资本 organizational capital

组织变革 organizational change

百事可乐 Pepsi

人事管理 personnel management

规划 planning

电源 power

价格敏感度 price sensitivity

定价 pricing

过程 process

产品检验 product inspection

产品生命周期 product life cycle

生产 production

生产部门 production department

生产成效 production effectiveness

生产效率 production efficiency

生产因素 production factor

产品 product

产品和服务 product and service

利润 profit

利润分享 profit-sharing

先进文化 progressive culture

促销 promotion

宣传 publicity

目的 purpose

质量目标 quality target

原料 raw material

招聘 recruitment

组织内部关系 relationships within organization

远程办公 remote working

报告期 reporting period

资源分配 resource allocation

资源规划 resource planning

资源 resources

零售企业 retail business

保留 retention

风险 risk

销售 sales

萨班斯法案 Sarbanes-Oxley Act

饱和度 saturation

分割 segmentation

甄选过程 selection process

自我评价 self-appraisal

服务企业 service businesses

服务 service

服务故障 service failures

服务营销 service marketing

设置目标和指标 setting objectives and targets

股价 share price

股份拥有 share-ownership

股东 shareholders

股份 shares

社会责任 social responsibility

社会经济类 socio-economic classes

社会学 sociology

员工纪律 staff discipline

员工晋升 staff promotion

人员编制 staffing

标准石油公司 Standard Oil (New Jersey)

股市 stock markets

战略约束 strategic constraints

战略目标 strategic objectives

战略选择 strategic options

管理学基础——原理篇
（注释版）

Management：the Basics   by Morgen Witzel

图字：01 - 2009 - 4719

ⓒ 2011 英文原版中文注释版专有出版权属经济科学出版社
版权所有　　不得翻印

策　　划：龚　勋
责任编辑：龚　勋　吴鹏昊